PARTIES *and* PROJECTS *for the* HOLIDAYS

CHRISTMAS WITH MARTHA STEWART LIVING

PARTIES and PROJECTS
for the
HOLIDAYS

Copyright © 2000
Martha Stewart Living
Omnimedia LLC
11 West 42nd Street,
New York, NY 10036
www.marthastewart.com

Originally published in book
form by Martha Stewart Living
Omnimedia LLC in 2000.
Published simultaneously by
Clarkson N. Potter, Inc., Oxmoor
House, Inc., and Leisure Arts.

A portion of this work was
previously published in
MARTHA STEWART LIVING.

Manufactured in the United
States of America.
Library of Congress Catalog
Number is available upon request.
ISBN 0-8487-1979-4 (hardcover)
0-8487-1980-8 (paperback)

Executive Editor: Kathleen Hackett
Deputy Editor: Alice Gordon
Text by Amy Conway
Art Directors: Linda Kocur and
Jill Groeber
Managing Editor: Molly Tully
Design Production: Jeanne Colgan
and Duane Stapp

CONTENTS

INTRODUCTION

For me, this holiday season means the good company of family and friends. In the days leading up to the actual festivities, we all like to spend time with one another making presents and decorations or cooking and baking dishes using treasured "heirloom" recipes. We welcome back our favorite rituals, such as finding and trimming the perfect tree, in which everybody, big and small, can participate. And we open our homes to allow everybody to gather and share in the delicious food and good cheer. This book is all about those wonderful holiday parties, projects, and recipes, with ideas to make them extra-special. ★ For the events in this book, we looked to memorable celebrations within our own *Martha Stewart Living* "family" of relatives, friends, and colleagues. At the tree-trimming buffet at my friend Salli LaGrone's charming cottage in Tennessee, a cocktail named after Salli's stepfather and dishes her grandmothers made were an important part of the meal. One of our food editors prepared roast goose with all the trimmings for a true holiday feast with her sister, their husbands, and their young sons. For Christmas Eve with my sister's family, we strung pinecones collected from the surrounding Maine woodlands to make beautiful rustic wreaths and garlands to decorate my beloved home, Skylands. One of my favorite gatherings is the "Candy Crafts with Kids" party with a few of our staff members, which was enjoyed by children and adults alike. Even the youngest child can join in and turn a few green gumdrops into a fanciful little Christmas tree. ★ Each family has holiday traditions its members come to expect every year, and while I encourage you to honor these customs, I hope you will create new ones as well. This season, use our book as a starting point for those new traditions. ★ Have the merriest Christmas and the happiest New Year.

Martha Stewart

GOOD MORNING *At this time of year, you can entertain at any meal. Here, my kitchen table in Westport is set for a small family breakfast. A pair of white-feather trees with classic cranberry garlands and miniature wreaths makes a pretty centerpiece. On the table, drabware cups are waiting to be filled with coffee and tea, and cranberry-glass stemware is ready for freshly squeezed juices and champagne. To make a garland, above left, string the berries directly onto floral wire, or use a thick needle and thread. For the wreaths, use wire, twisting the ends together to make a circle.*

part 1

THE PARTIES

THROW OPEN
YOUR DOORS
TO FAMILY
AND FRIENDS
THIS SEASON
FOR CASUAL
GATHERINGS
OR FANCY
DINNERS, AND
GLORY IN THE
GOOD CHEER

TRIMMING
THE
TREE
in
TENNESSEE

In most houses, the weeks leading up to Christmas are almost as magical as the day itself. There are halls to deck, gifts to wrap, and cookies to bake, so the merriment is usually in full swing long before the clock strikes midnight on December 24. The preparations are all

the more meaningful when you invite friends and family to share them with you. Bringing home the perfect evergreen calls for just such a celebration. ★ Guests at a tree-trimming party will appreciate being rewarded for their efforts with some of your best holiday cooking. At Salli LaGrone's Queen Anne—style cottage in central Tennessee, the enticements include

oyster pie, country ham, beaten biscuits, and pecan rolls. Like many southerners, Salli, a special-events and design consultant, celebrates her heritage with food and thinks of her recipes as family heirlooms. ★ "She's a wonderful cook," says Martha, who met her in the seventies, when Salli was put in charge of the food and decorations for the preview party of a big Nashville antiques show

A STATELY CEDAR *Martha and Salli bring their chosen tree through the front door of the 1880s Queen Anne—style cottage. More friends will come by to trim the tree and enjoy a southern feast. Opposite: The finished tree sparkles with handmade ornaments. Salli takes a playful approach to decorating, both for the season (by draping garlands over frames) and throughout the year (by upholstering a traditional slipper chair in vintage mattress ticking).*

called Heart of Country. She invited Martha, then a caterer, to act as a consultant at the event. "We flipped apple fritters all night long," says Salli. They also found that they share a love of food, antiques, and decorating, and they have been good friends ever since. ★ By the time guests arrive, Salli's cottage is already warm and welcoming, done up in the holiday style she is known for, with natural decorations made of greenery, fruit, and flowers. Each year, she forages for what she calls "roadsidea grandiflora," collecting blown-down branches and taking snippings from her friends' gardens as well as her own backyard. Salli augments these found and borrowed treasures with a few special purchases from the florist, then weaves the eclectic elements together, surprising even herself with decorations that are different each year. ★ For the buffet, Salli and Martha choose serving pieces from Salli's extensive collections of old silver and white ironstone. In front of the fireplace, they set out an extravagant selection of desserts. The tree is bare—at first. Salli's friends and neighbors take turns choosing shimmering ornaments to fill in the branches, passing a relaxing afternoon of chatting and eating, affirming old friendships, and starting new ones. At the end of the day, when the cottage finally quiets down, the tree is shining brightly, as if emanating the warmth that lingers after friends are gone.

FESTIVE WELCOME *A charming little bar facing the front door (opposite) greets guests, as does Salli's black Labrador retriever, Aggie. The nineteenth-century pitcher is filled with Maestro's Old-Fashioneds, bourbon-based cocktails named for Salli's stepfather, who gave her the recipe; the pitcher itself was a Christmas present from Martha. Guests can also help themselves to red or white wine from pretty decanters, dressed up with tiny wreaths for the holidays. The Kentucky tilt-top tea table is one of Salli's many regional antiques; collecting is among her passions.*

Maestro's old-fashioneds

*wild-mushroom pâté
with toast points*

oyster pie

*baked country ham
with beaten biscuits*

*marinated green bean
and butter bean salad*

citrus salad

*chicken hash over
toasted corn bread*

*Grandmother Miller's
pecan rolls*

*Freedom Hall
chocolate beet cake*

Nana's Japanese fruitcake

Salli's cranberry tartlets

steamed persimmon puddin

gingerbread angels

HOLIDAY SPARKLE *Silver-plated tinsel called lametta, this page, is easy to twist into shapes for handmade ornaments. Opposite, clockwise from top left: Martha finds just the right branch. Salli collects antique julep cups; the mushroom pâté is from a recipe she has relied on for years. Clemé Barkley hangs an ornament while Parker Schooley selects one for Hunter Kay. Aidan Rogers plays hide-and-seek behind the tree topper.*

A SOUTHERN FEAST *Salli loves to cook traditional dishes for Christmas (opposite); she uses her white iron-stone all year-round. Small wreaths of white tallow berries, cedar and green pepperberries, and red seam binding are suspended from a cedar wreath over the buffet. On the gilt wall bracket sits a champagne flute Salli has filled with lilies and surrounded with tiny crab apples. This page, clockwise from top left: A steamed persimmon pudding makes a homey holiday dessert. Friends who stop by include (back, from left) Litchfield Carpenter, Washington Dender, Martha, Parker, Mary and Hank Brockman, and Hunter Kay; in front are Salli, Clemé, and Salli's dog Miro. The recipe for the layer cake was handed down to Salli from her paternal grandmother, who called it "Japanese fruitcake," though no one is sure why. Martha and Salli admire the tree while Miro naps.*

TASTING MENU *A guest's plate includes a little of everything from the buffet: chicken hash over corn bread, butter beans and green beans, pickled okra, biscuits with country ham, oyster pie, and citrus salad. Opposite: Salli favors natural decorations, such as these Gloriosa lilies, apples, pears, and crab apples. Japanese fruitcake, a three-layer spice cake, commands a prime spot on the mantel; below are cranberry pies, pecan rolls, and gingerbread angels dancing around a moist chocolate cake.* FOR CRAFTS, SEE THE PROJECTS. FOR FOOD, SEE THE RECIPES.

CANDY
CRAFTS
with
KIDS

Gather a group of children at Christmas time, give them every shape, size, color, and flavor of gumdrops, licorice twists, and hard candies; and what will they do? Make ornaments, wreaths, and garlands, of course. Okay, so they'll pop a few pieces into their mouths along the way.

Once taught a few simple techniques, though, children will show as much interest in making things with candy as in gobbling it up. ★ Set up a table with bowls of candy and simple supplies, and children will work like elves for hours, turning gumdrops and other candies into intricate figures and impressive decorations. "You just cut part of a gumdrop off so there's a sticky side, then stick it to the next gumdrop," explains 9-year-old Mary Jane Young. That's pretty much all there is to it. ★ When they're ready to take a break, have ready some wholesome, savory food, like homemade macaroni and cheese, piglets in blankets, and peanut-butter-and-jelly sandwiches. We made particularly playful versions of these favorites—they are competing with candy, after all.

SWEET CELEBRATION
Santa (opposite) and a little girl bundled up with a muff are made from gumdrops, either cut or gently squeezed into shape, and licorice twists, with nonpareils for eyes. This page: Tom Young with his aunt, Kathleen Hackett, donned an apron and set to work creating a car out of candy. "I saw the Lifesavers and thought I could use them for wheels," he said.

LICORICE GARLANDS *Most kids know licorice twists are hollow in the middle—who hasn't used one as a straw?—which makes them easy to turn into garlands. Just cut the licorice into pieces and string onto sturdy thread, as Eileen Milman (above and top right) does here with orange and red twists. Tooth-picks are essential tools for candy projects (above right); use them to scrape away sugar on gumdrops so their surfaces will be sticky enough to adhere to other sweets. Opposite: Candy ornaments and garlands share branches with favorite old decorations; gumdrop topiaries line the sill behind the Christmas tree.*

CANDY FOREST *Red gumdrop topiary Christmas trees (below left) are planted in milk-glass pots adorned with polka-dot ribbon. Ivy Menderson and Andrés Fernández (below right) make more topiaries using toothpicks that have been broken in half to join the soft candies to foam-core cones. Ivy's brother, Cole (bottom right), works on a gumdrop bird with licorice wings. Opposite: Ball-style topiaries (right) have candy-cane stems; the "soil" in their pots consists of hard candies. Mary Jane Young makes a multicolored topiary (left, top and bottom); she took immediately to the candy craft. "I wouldn't call it easy or hard," she says. "I'd just call it fun."*

Christmas sandwiches
macaroni and cheese
piglets in a blanket
chocolate-bar hot chocolate

TIME FOR LUNCH *Macaroni and cheese (opposite, top left) seems even yummier when made with curly noodles and baked in single portions; mini hot dogs baked in store-bought crescent-roll dough make delectable piglets in blankets. Opposite, clockwise from top right: Ivy and Cole's mom, Heather MacIsaac, serves lunch. PB&Js are fit for a Christmas party when the top slices of bread are cut with holiday cookie cutters. Eileen tells Mary Jane a secret. This page: Candy-cane stirs give hot chocolate a minty taste. Leftover bread cut-outs are perfect for cinnamon toasts.*

SUGAR SCENES *Colorful ornaments look especially charming against the snow-white branches of a feather tree. Opposite: The adults will sit down for a bite to eat, while the kids sip hot chocolate and put finishing touches on their ornaments. The just-decorated tree makes an excellent centerpiece for the table.*

FOR CRAFTS, SEE THE PROJECTS.
FOR FOOD, SEE THE RECIPES.

CHRISTMAS
EVE
in
MAINE

When the ground is blanketed with snow and tiny icicles glisten from the tips of tree branches, it ought to be especially warm and welcoming indoors. There's nothing cozier than a Christmas Eve dinner with just a handful of guests, as Martha and five of her favorite people

discover while spending the holidays tucked into her house in Maine. Together, this group—Martha, her sister Laura Plimpton, and Laura's husband, Randy; their two sons, Charlie and Christopher; and Alison, Christopher's closest friend since kindergarten—decorate, cook, and enjoy the intimacy of their small gathering and the splendor of the setting. ★ Martha

is taken with the natural beauty of this part of the world, and the dense forest of towering evergreens surrounding her old stone house has given her ideas for decorating projects. Everyone participates, settling in front of the fireplace to wire, glue, and string together pinecones, making wreaths, ornaments, garlands, even centerpieces for the table. A group effort like this is an ideal activity

FIRESIDE COMFORT
Christmas stockings made from remnants of antique ingrain carpets are hung over the stone fireplace (opposite), before which Martha and her family spend much of their holiday. Handmade pinecone ornaments and garlands decorate the mantel and tree. The hand-blown glass balls on the table near the sofa are old fishing buoys, which Martha collects. This page: Martha's nephew Charlie Plimpton falls asleep waiting for Santa.

for the morning—it takes everyone's minds off the distracting stacks of presents beneath the majestic spruce standing in the corner. ★ In contrast to the rustic charm of the pinecone decorations, simple arrangements of red roses in the dining room are lush and opulent. Alison sets a formal dinner table with delicate cranberry-glass stemware and pink transferware plates and platters. The feast Martha and Laura are preparing is also elegant—when you're cooking for a small group, it's easier to devote more time (and money) to certain special dishes. Together, the two sisters roll out dough, slice apples paper-thin, and wait for the huge pot of water to come to a boil—lobster being a must on the menu in Maine. ★ The meal begins with hors d'oeuvres in the living room, where everyone can admire the tree as they nibble on shrimp-salad rolls and smoked-scallop hors d'oeuvres. When they take their places at the table, they indulge in a rich appetizer of lobster Newburg. The main course, a regal crown roast, is served alongside fresh green beans and fancy twice-baked potatoes brimming with savory soufflé-like fillings. Everyone somehow manages to save room for dessert, moist chocolate cake and a wonderful English confection called lardy cake, made with layers of pastry and dried fruit. ★ After dinner, young Charlie writes a note to Santa in his best penmanship and leaves it on the mantel. Martha adds a glass of milk and big cookies with chunks of chocolate and toffee to thank Mr. Claus for finding his way to this family waiting deep in the snowy woods of Maine.

MENU

lobster Newburg

endive petals
with smoked scallops

shrimp-salad rolls

finnan-haddie canapés

crown roast

creamy red and
green cabbage

warm green-bean salad

twice-baked potatoes
with spinach and
parsnip soufflés

lardy cake

chocolate-applesauce cake

Torie's chocolate-chunk
toffee cookies

REGAL TABLE *Crown roast of pork is an impressive Christmas Eve main course that is surprisingly easy to make (especially if you ask your butcher to trim and prepare the meat—the rib-chop section of a rack of pork). Opposite: The garland of balsam, yellow arborvitae, and rosehips plays off the pink of the place settings for a subtle holiday palette. A Venetian-print cloth covers the table, which is set for six with Art Deco cranberry-glass stemware and pink transferware. Cranberry-glass compotes are piled high with pinecones. Seventeenth-century Italian chairs with silk-velvet seat cushions await the dinner guests.*

MAKING MERRY *Alison Benton (top left) adds another present to the already overflowing pile beneath the tree. Center: Laura and Martha enjoy the meal they made together. Clockwise from top center: Appetizer portions of lobster Newburg—big chunks of the sweet, tender meat in a butter sauce flavored with sherry—are served in ramekins.*

Martha's lardy cake was inspired by a visit to a bakery in Gloucestershire, England. Charlie checks back in with his father after dinner. Lengths of wide ribbon with notched ends are gently folded as beds for place cards. The plate's pretty rim barely peeks out beneath the crown roast, twice-baked potatoes filled with parsnip and spinach soufflés, green-bean salad, and creamy cabbage.

HOLIDAY BOUNTY *The feast is presented on the seventeenth-century Spanish sideboard in transferware serving dishes (below). Martha's favorite piece is the platter set over a copper basin filled with hot water, which keeps the roast warm. Red roses are fragrant and beautiful; a few evergreen sprigs add a nice textural contrast. Right: Even Chin Chin the chow is dressed up for the holidays.*

PICTURE PERFECT *Randy, Charlie, Laura, Martha, and Christopher gather for a photograph beside the tree. Opposite: A chocolate cake made with applesauce and apple brandy is topped with a cider glaze, apple chips, and crystallized ginger.* FOR CRAFTS, SEE THE PROJECTS. FOR FOOD, SEE THE RECIPES.

CHRISTMAS
DINNER
in
MANHATTAN

It is almost instinctive, the way we return to familiar rituals at Christmas. Yet even the most beloved customs grow and evolve over time, just as families do. Stephana Bottom, senior food editor of *Martha Stewart Living*, usually spends the holidays with her sister, Allison, and their husbands

and young sons in the small Texas town where the sisters grew up. When they break with habit to celebrate at home in New York City, they weave together new ideas with favorite traditions. The main course is roast goose, the Christmas feast both Stephana's and Allison's husbands enjoyed when they were young. The poinsettia theme evokes the sisters' hometown, where the cheerful plants grow outdoors. Having the tree in the dining room adds to the sparkle of the holiday table. The boys, dizzy with excitement, play with toys from their stockings, while their parents sip champagne and prepare dinner at a leisurely pace, relishing the best Christmas tradition of all, the one that never changes: being with people you love.

DINNER BY THE TREE
Garlands grace the windows of the Manhattan dining room where the Christmas tree stands (opposite). There will be adults and children at this table, so it is set festively but not formally. Stephana serves dinner family style—which is appropriate since she's joined today by her close relatives. Her nephew Austin plays with Lily, the kitten. Above: The more ribbons, the more fun a present is to unwrap.

CHAMPAGNE AND STOCKINGS *A simple stocking topped with a wide ribbon cuff (opposite) is reserved for the youngest member of the family, kitten Lily. It contains, among other goodies, a catnip mouse, treats, and a new collar. This page, clockwise from top left: Champagne is for adults only, but everyone snacks on the toast fingers with blue cheese, pears, and pecans. Fabric poinsettias stay beautiful year after year; this wreath is made from wide ribbon in luscious pinks and reds. Stephana's son, Theo, opens his stocking while still in his pajamas; when there are children about, "every single thing about Christmas is more fun," says Stephana. The tree is decorated with ornaments embellished with glitter and more poinsettias.*

MENU

pear pecan toasts
garlic thyme popovers
crispy Waldorf salad
roast goose
brussels sprouts
with red onions
holiday fig roll
dried-fruit compote
Christmas cupcakes

OLD AND NEW TRADITIONS *The dining-room table, set with an eclectic mix of hotel silver, majolica, lustreware, and colored glass (opposite), proves that everything need not match—even for Christmas dinner. The centerpiece is roast goose, a deliciously tender bird, garnished with kumquats and pears and accompanied by wild-rice dressing. Side dishes also include brussels sprouts cooked with bacon and pearl onions, and a refreshing salad of fennel, grapes, apple, escarole, and pecans, which is inspired by the old-fashioned Waldorf salad; Allison's husband, Thaddeus, contributes his family's recipe for airy popovers, made with a touch of goose fat. This page: For dessert there's a fig roll (above left): a dense cake filled with creamy mascarpone and topped with candied kumquats. Stephana, Theo, Austin, and Allison at the table (top right). After dinner, Stephana's husband, Duncan, and nephew Austin (above right) blow out the candle in a handmade sconce.*

FOR CRAFTS, SEE THE PROJECTS. FOR FOOD, SEE THE RECIPES.

OPEN
HOUSE
on
NEW
YEAR'S
DAY

New Year's Eve, with its noisemakers, confetti, and flurries of midnight kisses, tends to outshine New Year's Day. But January 1 has its own kind of glow. With everyone pleasantly fatigued from the season's nonstop celebrations—but still in the mood for more—it is the

perfect time for an open house, which may be the most relaxed of all kinds of parties. The typical house has already been dressed up, so a host need only consider the food. Simple, homey dishes are what most of us crave after the excesses of the holidays. For this party, Frances Boswell, deputy food editor of *Martha Stewart Living*, planned a menu to please any palate, with

varied dishes that can be prepared in advance and will hold up beautifully—a few discreet trips to replenish platters is the only running around necessary. Some guests will just pop in for a drink (hair of the dog, anyone?) and a quick bite; others will sink deep into the sofa, not budging except for another visit to the buffet. And that's the most effort anyone should have to expend on this luxuriously lazy day.

FRESH START *Friends and neighbors gladly brave the cold and snow to come to a casual open house on the first day of the new year. Greet them with wreaths and garlands (opposite), which hold up best when displayed outside. These wreaths are acacia and tallow berry; the garland is acacia alone. Candles in hurricane lanterns illuminate the path after the sun goes down. This page: Martha arrives with a bucket of excellent apples.*

SEASONAL GREETING *A wreath made from silver-dollar eucalyptus and eucalyptus seeds is suspended over the informal little bar, where guests choose from bloody or virgin Marys or pear-and-champagne punch. Opposite, clockwise from top left: Camembert with warm sautéed pears is a star hors d'oeuvre. Others include stuffed celery, toast stars with lentils, smoked salmon, sun-dried-tomato palmiers, and cheese-and-poppy strudel. Bundled flatware is convenient for a buffet: these napkins are cinched with pink ribbon and adorned with a blossom. Kelli Ronci brings a wrapped baking pan of cookies to add to the dessert table. A sprightly but delicate flower arrangement decorates a side table.*

HOMESTYLE *Frances brings choucroute garni to the buffet. This hearty, unpretentious food is a welcome change after fancy holiday meals. Literally translated as "garnished sauerkraut," it is made by simmering meats such as slab bacon, pork butt, and sausages with potatoes and sauerkraut in a flavorful broth. Opposite: The key to creating a beautiful buffet is using serving dishes of varying heights; the tiered stand with hors d'oeuvres provides a naturally off-center focal point. Small flower arrangements add more height and color but won't get in the guests' way.*

MENU

pear-champagne punch

pear chips

holiday bloody Mary

avocado grapefruit salad

sun-dried tomato palmiers

smoked-salmon and
caramelized-onion celery stalks

twice-baked cheese strudel

Camembert with
pears and walnuts

lentil stars

choucroute garni

boeuf bourguignon

wild-mushroom and
spinach lasagna

pear tart

caramelized lemon tart

bar cookies

A TOOTHSOME BUFFET

Guests make their own salad (opposite) from lettuce, red onion, grapefruit sections, chunks of avocado, and pomegranate seeds; dressings are spicy lime vinaigrette and oil and vinegar. Vegetarian lasagna (this page, top right) layers pasta with wild mushrooms spiked with Madeira wine, fresh spinach with ricotta, and a creamy sauce. Clockwise from above right: Guests Eric Pike and Neje Bailey make their way around the buffet. Tiny wreaths encircle votive holders on the mantel. Boeuf bourguignon, the classic French beef stew made with Burgundy wine, is given a delicious, albeit untraditional, topping of mashed Yukon gold potatoes; presenting a serving dish atop an overturned one is both attractive and functional: The bottom dish acts as a trivet. All of the food from the buffet is easy enough to eat from a plate balanced on one's lap. Center: "Fortune tellers" are fitting for a party on January 1, when everyone is thinking of the year ahead; these paper creations are folded but left blank, so guests can fill in fortunes they want to tell.

SWEET AND SAVORY
*Dessert is set out at the same
time as the rest of the food.
At an open house, guests stop
by at different times, and their
appetites vary accordingly:
Some just want a snack or some-
thing sweet. Here they can
choose from a lemon tart with
a "bruléed" top; bar cookies,
including rugelach, pecan-
caramel shortbread, apricot
lattice cookies, and congo bars;
and a rustic tart with a
double crust and pear-butter
filling. The dessert buffet is
also the perfect place for the
most delectable cheeses.
A whole wheel of Stilton serves
dozens of guests; a Stilton
scoop is used to dig out the
soft, blue-veined cheese.*

HAPPY ENDINGS

This page from top: Linda Kocur tells her niece Kelly Snitko's fortune. Stilton is often paired with fruit and goes wonderfully with the pear tart. A peek inside a favor box reveals golden popcorn squares nestled in waxed tissue. Every bite of the lemon tart is sweet and tangy, crunchy and creamy, all at once; rugelach is usually crescent-shaped, but these, with a cream-cheese crust and chocolate-and-walnut filling, are baked in a pan, then cut into bars. Opposite: Plain lidded cardboard boxes are covered with paper, given a ribbon handle through a grommet in the top, and filled with cookies for guests to take home at the end of the day.

FOR CRAFTS, SEE THE PROJECTS.
FOR FOOD, SEE THE RECIPES.

part

part 2

THE PROJECTS

HOLIDAY
DECORATIONS
FOR THE TREE,
THE TABLE,
THE MANTEL
(AND EVEN
THE PRESENTS)
SHINE MORE
BRIGHTLY
WHEN YOU
MAKE THEM
YOURSELF

tasseled **teardrop**
beaded cage
flat eight-pointed **star**
three-dimensional **star**
tree **topper**
circular snowflake
beaded **snowflake**
tinsel-trimmed ornaments

Tinsel and Cookie Ornaments

Tinsel was once spun from pure silver and gold. Today's metallic strands are usually made from humbler materials, but you can still find tinsel that recalls its precious roots. It's called lametta and is imported from Germany, where tinsel was first made for Christmas decorations in the early 1600s. Because lametta is silver-plated, it tarnishes from a bright shine to a soft glow. These ornaments combine tinsel of various thicknesses with beads salvaged from vintage garlands; they'll look like family heirlooms the moment you complete them. Tufted along a wire base, lametta is easy to work with; just snip it into lengths and twist it as desired (it also comes in ready-made shapes, including a teardrop, as seen on this page). Look for vintage beads at tag sales and in your own boxes of holiday decorations. For assembly you'll need thin silver-colored wire, a hot-glue gun, craft or fabric glue, needle-nose pliers, and wire snippers or scissors you don't mind dulling.

tasseled teardrop

You will need a 5-inch-long tinsel teardrop, wire snippers or scissors, angel's-hair tinsel, thin wire, and beads.

1. This ornament (opposite top) starts with a 5-inch-long tinsel teardrop (right). Snip off wire loop at top.
2. Twist top to make a bottom-heavy figure eight.
3. For tassel, make a small bundle of 2½-inch lengths of angel's-hair tinsel by wiring them together at centers. Leave wire ends long.
4. Fold angel's hair so ends are aligned; bind top by wrapping wire around the bundle several times. Send wire ends through a bead, and pull bead down to hide wrapping around tassel top.
5. Position bead just below bottom of teardrop; twist wires around teardrop to secure.
6. Send wire ends through more beads, then twist wires around teardrop top (below top loop) to secure.
7. Twist wire into a hook, and trim excess.

beaded cage

You will need two 5-inch-long tinsel teardrops, wire snippers or scissors, hot glue, thin wire, a nail, and beads.

1. This ornament (opposite bottom) is made from two tinsel teardrops; snip the small wire loops from the tops of both (right).
2. Insert one teardrop inside the other, forming a cage; secure at top and bottom with hot glue.
3. Wrap the center of a length of wire around a nail several times, forming a little coil. Remove nail.
4. Press wire ends together; send them through a bead.
5. Position bead just below bottom of teardrop. Twist wires around teardrop to secure. Add several more beads to the wires.
6. Twist wires around the teardrop top to secure. Twist the wire ends into a hook, and trim excess.

flat eight-pointed star

*You will need lametta, hot glue, beads, thin wire, and
wire snippers or scissors.*

1. To make the star (above), bend lametta seven
times at 1½-inch intervals (right).

2. Bring ends together to make four-pointed star; join
with dab of hot glue. Repeat to make a second star.

3. Glue one star on top of the other, with points
alternating. To add a bead in the center, lace the
end of a piece of wire through an "elbow" in the star's
interior, then bring the wire ends together, and send
them through the bead. Secure wire ends to the
opposite interior elbow, and snip excess wire.

three-dimensional star

You will need lametta, hot glue, beads, thin wire, and wire snippers or scissors.

1. To make this three-dimensional star (opposite, right), bend 12½-inch length of lametta at 1¼-inch intervals (above).

2. Bring ends together to make a star shape, and join them with hot glue. Make a second star.

3. Insert one star inside the other, so they are perpendicular to each other, and secure with glue where they meet. To add a bead in the center, send the end of a piece of wire through the elbow where the two stars meet. Bend the wire ends together, and send them through the bead. Then secure the wire ends to the opposite elbow of the star, and twist the ends into a hook. Trim excess wire.

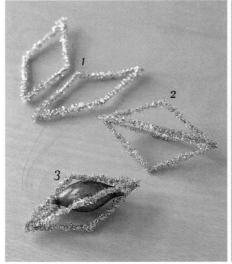 

tree topper

You will need lametta, hot glue, thin wire, and beads.

1. To make this tree topper (top right), form 2-inch-long diamond shapes from lametta, securing the ends with hot glue (above). We used twenty diamonds in all.

2. Insert one diamond into another, making a cage, and glue at top and bottom. Repeat, making ten cages.

3. To wire a bead into each cage, wrap the center of a piece of wire around one point of the cage. Have the wire ends hang down into the cage. Send the ends through a bead, preferably an elongated one (or use several smaller beads), then secure ends to opposite point of cage.

4. Wire the cages together at their "elbows."

5. Coil lametta into a flat disk large enough to fill the hole in the middle of all the joined cages.

6. Glue the coil into place. To put the topper on the tree, send two ends of a length of wire through the coil, and twist the ends around the topmost tree branch.

circular snowflake

You will need lametta, a pencil, thin wire, pliers, beads, and wire snippers or scissors.

1. Leaving a long tail, wind a length of lametta once around a pencil to make an eyelet; repeat at 1-inch intervals, making eight eyelets.
2. Form tinsel into a circle; wrap loose end around whole circle, doubling its thickness.
3. Thread four lengths of wire through four eyelets; send ends through beads. Bend ends with pliers to hold beads in place. Trim excess on all but one; bend it into a tiny hook.

beaded snowflake

You will need lametta, wire snippers or scissors, thin wire, beads, and pliers.

1. For this ornament, we used lametta with a wavy silhouette.
2. Snip three lengths of lametta to include two of its "bumps."
3. Twist lengths together at their centers, then reinforce the hub with wire. Curve each of the spokes. Thread a bead onto end of each spoke, and with needle-nose pliers, bend each end into a tiny hook to keep bead in place.

tinsel-trimmed ornaments

You will need wallpaper, fabric, or printed paper; card stock; craft glue; vellum; sheets of plastic; scissors; hot glue; lametta; and beads.

1. Reinforce a pretty patterned material, such as wallpaper, fabric, or sheet music, by sandwiching card stock between two layers of it. Join the layers by brushing with craft or fabric glue; we added an outer layer of vellum on each side (leave off vellum if using fabric), making five layers. Let dry. Make a template out of flexible plastic (the lid of a disposable food container, a plastic folder, or the like) using one of the holiday shapes on the following page. Position shape on layered material, trace, and cut out.

2. Hot-glue tinsel around edge of shape, using glue sparingly and slowly.

3. Add embellishments if you wish. This bell (bottom left) was given a jingle bell. The half-moon (center right) has a tiny star dangling from one point.

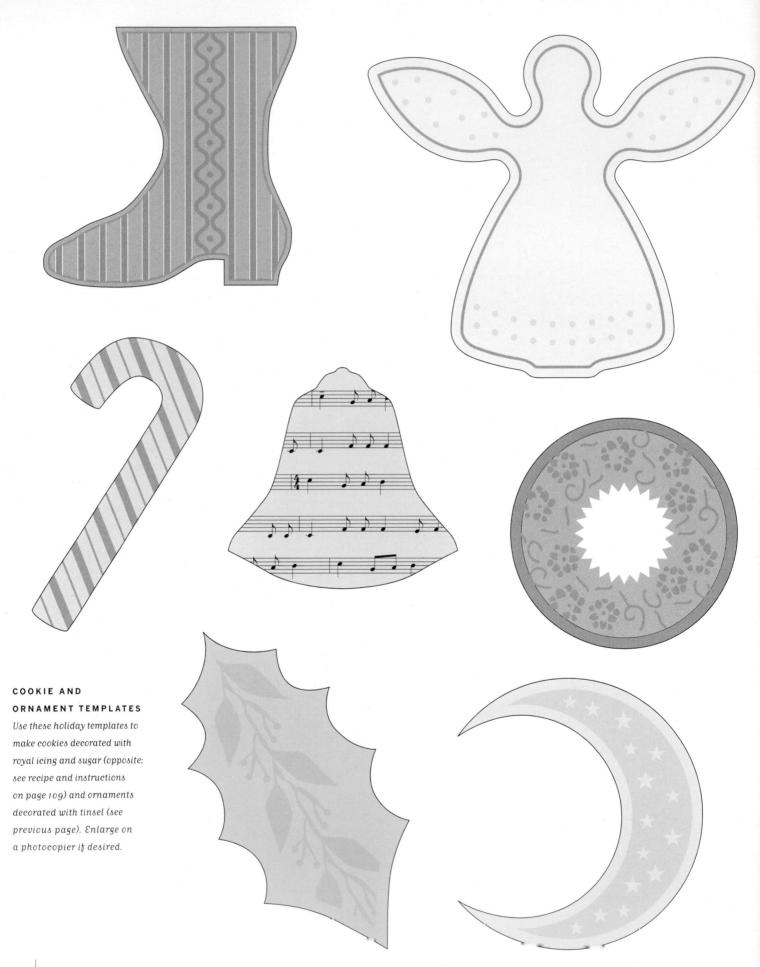

COOKIE AND ORNAMENT TEMPLATES

Use these holiday templates to make cookies decorated with royal icing and sugar (opposite; see recipe and instructions on page 109) and ornaments decorated with tinsel (see previous page). Enlarge on a photocopier if desired.

gumdrop and licorice garlands

gumdrop ornaments

gumdrop balls

gumdrop topiaries

Decorating With Candy

Talk about a winter wonderland: These candy creations—Christmas trees, Santa Claus, and little girls and boys—look like they've come from a magical place where it snows sugar and everything is made of sweets. It's hard to believe how easy they are for kids (or adults) to create. Gumdrops are as malleable as modeling clay, soft enough to slice with a plastic knife, and so sticky they adhere to one another without the help of glue or hardware. They make perfect, plump mini people, accessorized with licorice twists and hard candies, as well as garlands and topiary-style decorations. Small, large, and crescent-shaped gumdrops can be found in a rainbow of colors in almost any grocery store. If you plan to use a single shade for larger creations (like our red gumdrop topiaries), you'll need to buy several bags and separate the colors. Even so, at a dollar or two per bag, this is hardly a pricey proposition. Pick up some fruit-flavored twists and some vibrant hard candies to expand the palette beyond the basic red and black of licorice. Your last stop is the baking aisle for nonpareils, sprinkles, or other edible decorations. If you end up with extra candy, don't worry—it isn't likely to go to waste.

gumdrop garlands

You will need gumdrops, licorice twists, scissors, a darning needle, and waxed twine or other thick thread.

Set out bowls with ingredients for the garlands (right, top): small gumdrops and twists cut into sections of varying lengths. Thread a darning needle with a one-yard length of waxed twine or other thick thread. Use the needle to string the candies onto the thread in a pleasing sequence (right, below); make another yard-long garland, tie it to the first one, and continue until you've reached the length you desire. Opposite: Any child would be delighted to have his or her own little tree decorated with handmade ornaments. Even though they're made of candy, the decorations aren't edible; not only do gumdrops become stale once displayed, but also the ornaments have wire or thread hangers, and the topiaries have toothpicks inside. So let the youngest members of the family know that these decorations are to be admired, not eaten.

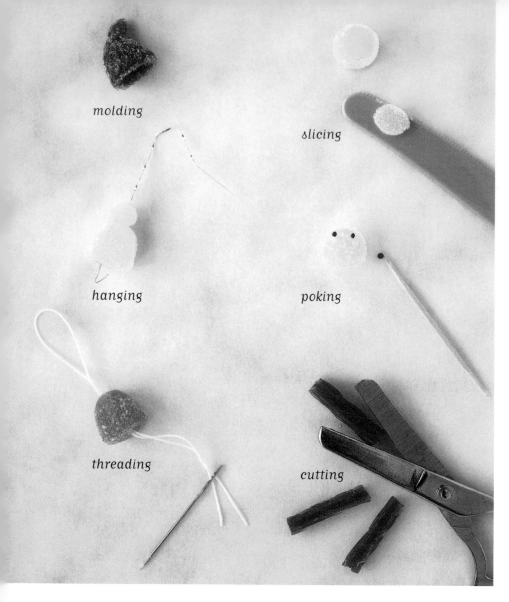

molding

slicing

hanging

poking

threading

cutting

gumdrop ball

You will need gumdrops, a darning needle, waxed twine, and a plastic knife.

The simple, cheerful ornament below demonstrates just how easy it is to work with these sweets: Thread a small gumdrop as shown at bottom. Slice off the end of another small gumdrop, and stick it to the threaded one, which will be at the center of the ornament. Continue slicing and sticking, adding gumdrops all around the first one.

MOLDING Gently use your fingers to flatten, stretch, or elongate gumdrops (whole ones or cut portions). The Santa hat, for example, started out as a small gumdrop. Start with soft gumdrops fresh from a closed bag, not ones that have been exposed to air, which stiffens them.

HANGING Add a wire hook to the piece that will be the top of the ornament, such as a hat, before you finish assembly. Push a wire through hat from bottom up through top so there's wire coming out at either end. Bend wire at bottom into small hook; push it into gumdrop to secure. Bend top portion into larger hook, for hanging.

THREADING This technique is used to hang the gumdrop ball: Send a darning needle threaded with waxed twine through a gumdrop, leaving a loop for hanging on one side. Knot loose ends on other side. Trim excess

SLICING Use a plastic knife to slice a gumdrop to change its shape, expose a sticky surface, or get a little piece for a detail. The knives will get gummy, so when not in use keep them in bowls of water, which dissolves the sugar and keeps your tools clean.

POKING Use a toothpick to make holes in gumdrops for adding parts like arms and legs, or for scraping away sugar for adding nonpareil eyes—then use a sticky toothpick to pick up those tiny decorations, and push into place.

CUTTING Kids' safety scissors are sharp enough to cut hollow twists into sections for garlands or thinner strips for arms, legs, and hair.

gumdrop topiaries

For topiaries, you will need gumdrops, 2-inch Styrofoam balls, small pots, toothpicks, a plastic knife, peppermint sticks, hot glue, hard candies, double-stick tape, and ribbon. For Christmas trees, you will need gumdrops, 4-to-6-inch Styrofoam cones, small pots with same diameter as Styrofoam cone, toothpicks, popsicle sticks, and a Styrofoam ball fitted to size of pot.

These trees can be made in a single color, a predetermined pattern, or a multicolored mix.

1. Break toothpicks in half, and poke pointed ends into foam; push small gumdrops onto exposed ends. With topiary, leave room for tree's trunk. With cone for Christmas tree, start at top.

2. To plant topiary in its pot, use a knife to carve out a hole in foam for a thick, striped stick of candy. Cut another foam ball in half, and make a matching hole in the flat side; place into pot. Hot-glue the stick candy to the topiary top, then push other end into foam in the pot. Hide foam with hard candies, like these peppermint pillows. Tie the pot with a ribbon. Use double-stick tape to hold ribbon in place.

3. For the Christmas-tree topiary, poke a popsicle stick into bottom of cone; make a cut through a Styrofoam ball half, and poke other end of stick through; place into pot. Add ribbon.

These candy diagrams show you the ingredients of the ornaments (left columns, this page and opposite); the order in which they're put together (center columns, this page and opposite); and the finished product (right columns, this page and opposite). See page 72 for techniques on working with gumdrops.

christmas eve in maine

pinecone wreath
mini pinecone garland
pinecone Christmas balls
pinecone and
snowflakes
tinsel snowflakes
fringe-cuff stocking
flower arrangements

Pinecones, Stockings, and Roses

When Christmas is on your mind, pinecones on the branches of conifers resemble ornaments that have been hung with care. It's no wonder that these gems of nature translate so easily into indoor holiday decorations. All pinecones, which protect seeds of conifers as they develop, share a similar structure, but they don't all look the same. Pinecones may be barrel-shaped, almost round, egg-shaped, or cylindrical; they may be as small as your thumb or as big as your fist. This diversity, along with the distinctive architectural design of pinecones, makes them immensely appealing for holiday projects. Use little cones for dainty garlands, turn large ones into a grand wreath, and combine shapes and sizes to create towering centerpieces and unique ornaments. (If you can't collect enough for your creations from your own yard, don't worry. You'll find them at craft stores.) Alongside woody pinecones, a few special arrangements of fresh flowers will look even more lush. Red roses, with their velvety petals and intoxicating aroma, are celebratory and romantic; perhaps even better, they're versatile and easy to work with. Pile them into unusual vessels for almost effortless holiday displays.

pinecone wreath

You will need pinecones, a double-wire wreath form, spray paint, floral wire, wire cutters, and ribbon.

This 3-foot wreath is made with natural and gold-painted pinecones. Gild cones with spray paint, or look for gold cones at craft stores. Fitting the pinecones onto the wreath form is like doing a jigsaw puzzle, so it helps to have cones in varying sizes. Wrap a length of floral wire around base of pinecone. Position cone on wreath form; twist wire ends around form to secure. Continue adding pinecones, making wreath as full as you desire. Tie a bow of wide satin ribbon. Poke a wire through back of bow; secure wire ends around wreath.

mini pinecone garland

You will need small pinecones, a T-pin, brown cording, a tapestry needle, and 6mm gold beads.

Use small pinecones for this garland (we used about sixteen tamarack pinecones per foot of garland). With a T-pin, poke a hole through each pinecone, from the base to the tip. Thread a tapestry needle with cording the length you'd like the finished garland to be. Thread the pinecones (each facing the same direction) onto the needle. Add a gold bead at every foot or at desired intervals. If you find working with one long strand unwieldy, make several shorter lengths, then tie the pieces together.

pinecone Christmas balls

You will need small pinecones, spray paint, Styrofoam balls, hot glue, and ribbon.

1. To cover a 3-inch Styrofoam ball, you will need about 100 small pinecones, such as tamarack or hemlock. If you want your ball to be studded with gold pinecones, spray-paint several cones, and let dry before starting. (Or use store-bought gold pinecones.) For an all-gold decoration, spray-paint entire ornament after it has been assembled. Dab hot glue onto Styrofoam ball; hold base of pinecone in place for a few seconds until glue hardens. Continue attaching cones snugly against one another in a ring around ball. Apply another ring, leaving no gaps. Continue attaching pinecones in rings until there's room for only one more pinecone at either end. Add a pinecone at one end, but leave gap at other. Knot together ends of a 6-inch length of thin ribbon (or longer for a longer loop). Dab hot glue onto knot; position knot on uncovered spot on ball. Glue a final pinecone into place over knot.

2. These finished balls are ready for hanging.

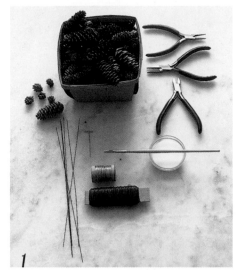

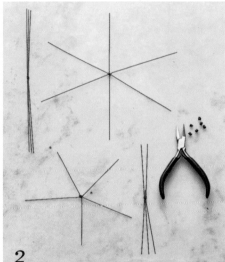

pinecone stars and snowflakes

You will need small pinecones, floral wire, round-nose pliers, wire cutters, white craft glue, a T-pin, needle-nose pliers, and 20-gauge brass wire.

1. For this project, look for small pinecones such as tamarack and white spruce.

2. Pinch the end of a 2-inch length of floral wire in round-nose pliers, and coil wire four times around the tip of pliers; trim off excess. Cut three equal lengths of straight floral wire (between 6½ and 9 inches, depending on the size you'd like the ornament to be). Hold lengths together, and thread through coil. Position coil at midpoints of lengths, and crimp tightly with round-nose pliers. Spread out wires so "spokes" of snowflake are evenly spaced. To make a five-pointed star, snip off one of the spokes close to the center, and bend wire inward to secure.

3. Pierce each pinecone from base to tip with T-pin.

4. Thread cones onto wire spokes, repeating same sequence on each spoke.

5. Repair any split pinecones with glue as you go. Glue a single pinecone to the center, hiding the coil. Wrap the end of each spoke around the tip of needle-nose pliers to make a small loop. Trim excess off remaining spokes. Bend brass wire into an ornament hanger, and hook onto one loop.

6. Here is a selection of completed five- and six-pointed stars.

tinsel snowflakes and garlands

You will need wired gold tinsel, pinecones, scissors or wire cutters, a drill press, brass wire, round-nose pliers, a tapestry needle, and ribbon.

1. Cut three 6½-inch lengths of wired gold tinsel (see page 45 for more about wired tinsel). Using pliers, twist together at midpoint. Cut a 15-inch length of tinsel. Wrap one end around one spoke of snowflake, 1 inch from tip. Crimp long piece of tinsel 1 inch from where it's joined to snowflake, forming an inverted V. Wrap tinsel around next spoke. Work your way around the snowflake, joining tinsel to the remaining spokes, making inverted Vs. Cut six 2½-inch lengths of tinsel. Twist each around a spoke, ½ inch from tips, forming Vs.

2. Modify technique for different designs. Make ornament hooks from brass wire.

3. For garland, we used red-pine cones. To make holes through larger pinecones like these, use a drill press.

4. Thread a tapestry needle with ⅜-inch-wide ribbon the length you want garland to be. Thread six pinecones onto ribbon. Attach a gold-tinsel snowflake: Join tip of one spoke to ribbon with twists of thin brass wire. Hold ribbon taut across back of snowflake, and fasten opposite spoke; fasten snowflake center to ribbon with more wire.

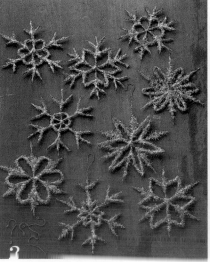

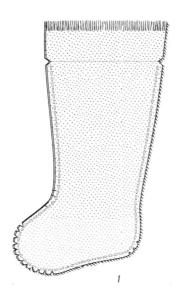

1

2

fringe-cuff stocking

You will need fabric, scissors, template (see page 87), and a sewing machine or needle and thread.

Use tapestry fabric with a loose weave for this stocking so you can unravel the cut edge with your fingers for a fringed cuff. The cuff is the top of the stocking folded over, not a separate piece, so make sure you like the way the fabric looks on both sides.

1. Enlarge the template on a photocopier to desired size. Cut out two stocking shapes from your chosen fabric. Pin the two pieces of fabric with right sides together, and stitch around the perimeter, starting at one notch on the template, going around the bottom of the stocking, and stopping at the other notch. Cut notches in the heel and foot so the stocking will lie flat when turned.

2. Turn right side out, and stitch up the sides of what will be the cuff. Fringe the top by pulling out threads with your fingers. Turn the cuff down. Use the same fabric or ribbon to add a loop for hanging.

temporary frogs

You will need ¼-inch white masking, floral, or artist's tape; and evergreen sprigs or flowers.

Here are two ways to hold flower stems in place, which is especially important when making arrangements in a wide-mouthed, shallow container like a footed compote or tureen.

1. Add water to vessel. Use narrow white tape to make a grid across opening. Strip leaves from flower stems, trim stems to proper length, and arrange in holes in grid, making sure flowerheads hide tape. Try not to get tape too wet as you work.

2. Layer evergreen sprigs into vessel, crisscrossing inside to form a web and letting tips drape over edges. Add water. Carefully poke flower stems into web, starting at edges before filling in center.

pinecone tower

You will need pinecones, hot glue, and spray paint.

Any shallow bowl or footed compote can be used for this decoration. Without glue, lay a few pinecones in the center of the bowl, and add pinecones around and on top of them to get a feel for how the cones fit together and the proportions of the tower you'll build. Disassemble. Lay two or three pinecones on their sides to make a base for the tower (above left). Use hot glue to join them. Return base to bowl, and continue gluing on cones one at a time, making complete layers before adding the next. When the tower is as tall as you want it to be, fill in gaps with tiny pinecones (above right). Some can be spray-painted gold if you wish (left).

COMING UP ROSES *Vases aren't the only vessels suitable for displaying flowers. Gather pitchers, tureens, footed dishes, even teacups for arrangements of roses (we added a few carnations and evergreen sprigs, too). The flowers appear to overflow a transferware pitcher and arch over the top of a tureen. Just a handful of roses fits into a teacup and footed tumbler. A single bloom floats in a delicate goblet.*

ribbon poinsettias and WREATH
napkin rings
ornaments
ribbon-cuff stocking
woven gifts
glittered ornaments
baking-pan sconces

Ribbon, Light, and Glitter

It's remarkable how ribbons weave their way into so many aspects of the holidays. As a little pre-Christmas gift to yourself, consider visiting a shop with a great supply and stocking up on lustrous lengths of satin, velvet, and other sumptuous cloth ribbons. They are more versatile than you might imagine (and they're also reusable—don't forget to save the beautiful ones that come your way). Wide ribbon strips can be cinched at their middles and wired into poinsettia shapes, which make wonderful wreaths, ornaments, and even napkin holders. They're almost as cheery as fresh poinsettias, but their vivid color won't fade come January. Ribbons are perfect cuffs for handmade stockings, too; since the sides of these fabric strips don't need hemming, the sewing is especially easy. Of course, presents must be adorned with ribbon—but why stop at a modest bow? Crisscross ribbons all over your parcels for gifts both lovely to behold and exciting to unwrap, one strand at a time. In this chapter, there are also a couple of ideas for crafts that don't call for ribbon. Glittered ornaments look charming on the tree with the cloth poinsettias. And we haven't figured out how to make candleholders from ribbon (yet), so we've used vintage baking pans instead.

ribbon poinsettias and wreath

You will need ribbon, pins, wire, fabric-covered wire, "pips" or beads, craft glue, floral wire, and a Styrofoam form.

1. To make ribbon poinsettia, cut a 10-inch length of 2½- to 4-inch-wide ribbon. Cut it diagonally into three diamonds. Pinch each diamond across short axis, to pleat, pin. Form six-petaled blossom with three diamonds. Secure with wire around centers, twisting in back; remove pins. Remove stems from "pips"— artificial stamens sold in craft stores—and glue to front of blossom (you can use beads instead). Or glue in stamens after poinsettias are attached to wreath.

2. Add leaves: Cut 5-inch lengths of 2- to 3-inch-wide green ribbon. With right side down, fold ribbon into sideways L shape. Make crease at middle of first fold as you bring upper leg of "L" to cover lower leg; edges will line up in a house shape. For wreath, pleat open end of house-shaped ribbon with your fingers; pin in place.

3. Shave edges of 19-inch Styrofoam form, making them rounder. Wrap with ribbon; pin ends. Attach poinsettias and leaves with straight pins, hiding pins within ribbon folds, overlapping blossoms as you go.

4. For leaves for napkin rings and ornaments, make ribbon house shapes as in step 2, with 1½-inch-wide ribbon. Coat tip of length of fabric-covered wire with glue; insert it into open end of shape. Cinch ribbon around wire end; secure with floral tape. Send other end of wire through wire on back of poinsettia; trim wire to desired length to wrap around napkins or branches for ornaments. Add second leaf to other end of wire.

POINSETTIA NAPKIN RINGS AND ORNAMENTS *Tabletop to tree: Ribbon poinsettias with wire stems are versatile. On the holiday table, they cinch napkins with style; on the tree, their soft petals add a lush touch and a burst of color. Use them year after year to decorate for the holidays; attach them to a simple garland hung around a doorway or wound around a banister, or fasten them to a pillow for a festive flourish.*

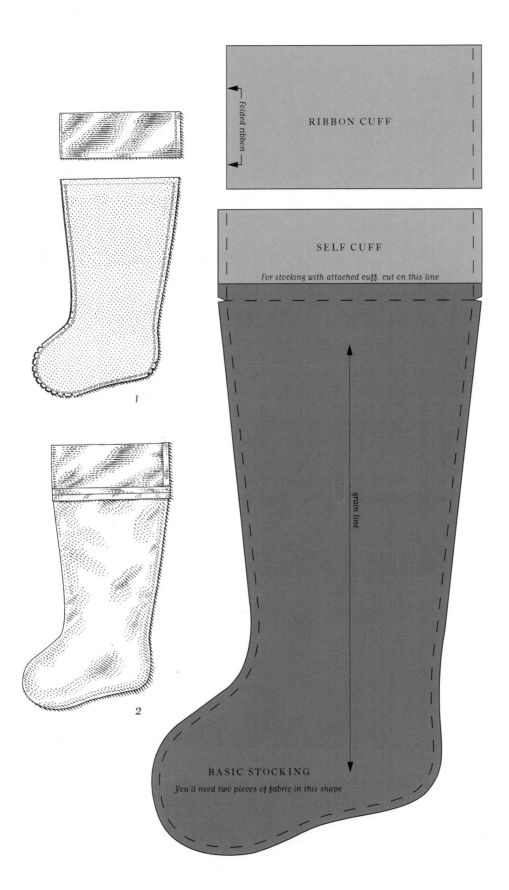

RIBBON CUFF

folded ribbon

SELF CUFF

For stocking with attached cuff, cut on this line

grain line

BASIC STOCKING

You'll need two pieces of fabric in this shape

1

2

ribbon-cuff stocking

You will need fabric, a wide ribbon, a sewing machine or needle and thread, and pins.

This sweet stocking is just about a foot long, with a cuff made from 2¾-inch ribbon, but you can alter the proportions. Enlarge stocking and cuff templates on a photocopier; use it to cut out two pieces of fabric such as the cashmere-wool blend we used.

1. Pin stocking pieces with right sides together; sew with ½-inch seam allowance, leaving the top open. For the cuff, cut length of ribbon twice as long as ribbon-cuff template. With ribbon folded in half, with right sides together, sew the cut ends together with ½-inch seam allowance, forming a loop, and trim the seam.

2. Turn stocking right-side out. Insert cuff inside stocking (with right side of cuff against inside of stocking); pin. Cut a length of thin ribbon or satin cord for a loop for hanging. Pin loop between cuff and stocking so ends are flush with top of cuff and stocking. Sew cuff, loop, and stocking together. Turn the cuff out. Hand-stitch poinsettia to stocking if you wish.

RIBBON SHEEN, CANDLE GLOW *Odd-shaped packages require ingenious wrapping (this page). Modify the woven-ribbon technique (page 90) for round tins by crisscrossing ribbons. On a triangular box, ribbons are trimmed and taped on two sides so they lie flat. The label of this wine bottle is hidden with ribbon; then more ribbons are wrapped from top to bottom. Opposite: Sconces fashioned from vintage baking pans (details, page 90) wash a wall in soft light; votives in fluted molds add to the effect.*

ribbon wrap

You will need paper; ribbon of different widths, colors and textures; and double-sided tape.

The holidays are a time to be generous with everything—including ribbons. Start by wrapping a box in solid-color paper. Then wrap a single ribbon around it, and secure the end of the ribbon with double-sided tape on the bottom of the box. Add a few more ribbons parallel to the first, mixing colors, widths, and textures as you wish. Next, interweave ribbons perpendicular to the first one, going over-under-over for one, then under-over-under for the next, and continue until box is finished.

glittered ornaments

You will need Christmas balls, glitter, craft glue, and a soft brush.

Customize dollar-a-dozen Christmas balls with an artful application of glitter. Garlands, holly, poinsettias, and candy canes are all festive motifs (opposite). A small bottle of craft glue with a fine-tipped applicator is the best tool for creating them. The trick is to add only one color glitter at a time; for example, for a candy cane, dab dots of glue in the shape of a cane, leaving spaces between the dots. Working over the bowl of glitter or a clean sheet of waxed paper to catch the excess, sprinkle with red glitter. Let the glue dry completely. Then use a soft brush to remove excess glitter. Fill in the gaps with more glue dots, and dust with silver glitter, creating a striped candy cane. Fine-textured glass glitter gives the best results.

baking-pan sconces

You will need baking pans, candles, candle clips, and plate hangers or nails.

Vintage baking pans with interesting shapes and textures are easy to turn into ingenious reflectors for flickering candles. Pans with a patina are even prettier than the shiniest ones. Look for old pans at flea markets, where they may cost less than a dollar apiece. To add a candle, just clip a candle-holder made for a Christmas tree to the bottom edge of the pan. Vintage candle clips are a good match, but new ones can be used as well. To hang the sconces on the wall, try plate hangers, or tap a nail right through the pan into the wall. Adhesive squares are strong enough to support most pans, but may leave a sticky residue behind.

votive **wreaths**

eucalyptus wreaths

eucalyptus **garland**

packing **cookies**

fortune tellers

Flourishes and Favors

A party should be special from start to finish. Here you'll find ideas for decorations that welcome guests to your house, a party activity to engage them, and favors to send them home with at the end of the day. At another time of year, you might fill the house with fresh flowers, but in winter, when choices dwindle and prices rise, it makes sense to rely mostly on greenery, so abundant and versatile, lush and fragrant. Weave sprigs of greenery into wreaths and garlands for the front door, banisters, and mantelpieces. Then go for the unexpected: A beautiful wreath can hang like art on a wall; a tiny one can encircle the neck of a decanter or perch atop a glass candleholder. A game or activity provides a party with a sense of fun and purpose, but it shouldn't dominate the day. "Fortune tellers," made from patterned origami paper, let guests predict the good things that are sure to come their way. They just might see cookies in one anothers' futures, if you bake extras to pack in pretty boxes as favors.

votive wreaths

You will need greenery and winter berries, floral wire, and wire cutters.

Wispy wreaths made from snippets of greenery and a few winter berries float like halos over glass votive holders and lanterns. The wreaths opposite are made with knife-blade eucalyptus and tallow berries; knife-blade eucalyptus with dried canella berries; acacia and tallow berries; and knife-blade eucalyptus and eucalyptus seeds. This page, near right: Cut a length of greenery long enough to wrap around the top of your candle holder, and cut a piece of wire about 1½ times that length. Leaving a little wire loose at the end, wrap the wire carefully around the greenery and the stem of a berry or cluster of berries, joining the berries to the greenery. Continue wrapping and adding berries, doing your best to keep the wire hidden in the greenery as you go. Far right: Wrap the mini garland around the top of the candle holder, and twist the excess wire ends together. Bend them into a little hook to hold the garland near the rim of the glass. For a simpler version (without berries), wind wire around greenery, wrap around the holder, and wire ends together, then make the wire hook.

making wreaths

You will need greenery, a double-wire wreath form (we used a 24-inch one), floral wire, a paddle, and wire cutters.

The technique for this wreath can be used for any kind of greenery and many different effects. We wired small bundles of knife-blade eucalyptus and eucalpytus seeds to a 24-inch wreath form for a narrow wreath with a delicate look. Secure floral wire on a paddle to a double-wire wreath form. Lay a bundle of greenery onto the form, and wrap the wire around the stems (above); do not cut the wire. Add another bundle, overlapping the first by about half, and wrap again. Continue wiring on bundles of greenery until you've worked your way around the wreath. Cut the wire, and secure to the form.

making garlands

You will need greenery, floral wire on a paddle, wire cutters, and twine.

Use this basic technique for any garland: The one at right is acacia, which is best for outdoors, since it quickly dries out and curls indoors. Secure floral wire on paddle to twine; lay bundle of greenery onto twine, and wrap wire around stems and twine (below); do not cut wire. Add second bundle, overlapping first by about half; wrap with wire. Continue until garland is desired length. Secure wire, and cut; trim twine ends. If you have a large work table, you might find it easier to tie one end of twine to a chair before starting; push chair up to table, stretch out twine, and work from chair across table.

tallow berries

dried canella
berries

eucalyptus
seeds

silver-dollar
eucalyptus

Italian
eucalyptus

knife-blade
eucalyptus

acacia

GREENERY GLOSSARY
*Here's a closer look at the
greenery and berries
used to make the garlands
and wreaths on these
pages. We chose these
for their varied shapes,
sizes, and colors, but you
don't have to search
for the exact plants we
used—across the country
there are trees, shrubs,
and vines with beautiful
leaves, needles, or berries
at this time of year, and
you can take snippings
from plants in your own
backyard. If you don't
have the raw material on
your property, visit Christmas-tree lots, florists,
garden centers, or your
neighbor's garden—with
permission, of course.*

cellophane wrap

You will need cellophane, cake rounds, cookies, and ribbon.

Cookies peek out enticingly from shiny cellophane, a festive wrap for favors. Use cake rounds, which you'll find at baking-supply stores, as "plates." Place a round on a large piece of clear cellophane. Arrange a little mountain of cookies on top. Gather the cellophane, and cinch with a cheerful ribbon.

ribbon-box favors

You will need boxes, waxed paper, a ruler, a utility knife, grommets, and a hammer.

Small square boxes are just the right size for a snack's worth of cookies. If making bar cookies, which are easy to turn out by the dozen, you might select your boxes first, then cut cookies to fit. Plain white boxes look pretty with colored-ribbon handles. You can also cover boxes with patterned paper or buy decorative boxes. To add a ribbon handle, trace two diagonal lines from corner to corner on top of lid. Where lines cross in center, use utility knife to cut round hole big enough for nose end of grommet (far left); insert nose end. Using a hammer, fasten other grommet half according to package directions. Erase pencil lines. Send ribbon ends through grommet; knot inside box top. Line box with waxed paper; fill with cookies.

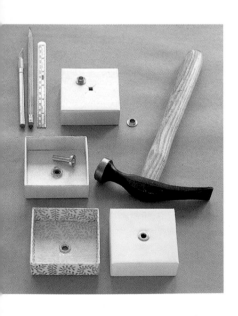

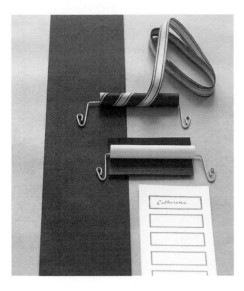

handle-box favors

You will need cardboard boxes, waxed paper, double-sided tape, ribbon, shopping-bag handles, and labels.

Give boxes shopping-bag handles so guests can tote them home with ease. Line box with waxed paper, and fill with cookies. Wrap decorative paper around the box, and tape on the bottom. Tie the box with ribbon. Cut a rectangle of paper as wide as a shopping-bag handle and just a little longer than its diameter. Wrap around handle, and attach with double-sided tape. Add a small adhesive label to or wind ribbon around the handle and fasten at ends with small pieces of double-sided tape.

cookie tin

You will need cookies, a baking tin, plastic wrap, colored paper, and ribbon.

As a gift to the host, bring along cookies to add to the buffet. These caramel-pecan shortbreads, apricot lattice cookies, rugelach fingers, and congo bars are arranged in a baking tin, which can be used long after the cookies are gone. Wrap tin in plastic wrap, then fold colored or patterned paper around it—this is book cloth, which has a fabriclike finish—and tie with a ribbon.

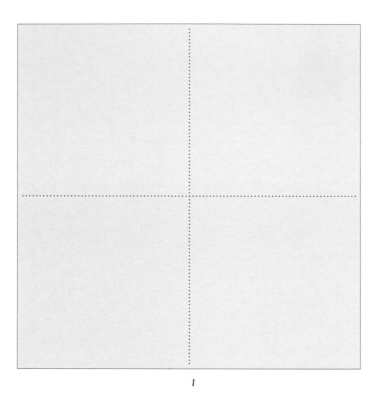

1

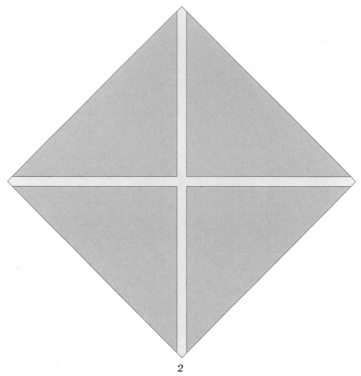

2

fortune tellers

You will need patterned origami paper and a bone folder or popsicle stick.

Patterned origami paper, so lovely and perfectly square, is ideal for making fortune tellers, but you can cut any paper into squares to use instead.

1. Fold a piece of paper in half, then in half again (it's best to fold widthwise and lengthwise, not diagonally, to avoid creases on the finished fortune teller).

2. Fold each of the four corners into the center, creating a smaller square.

3. Turn the paper over and fold the corners into the center again, creating an even smaller square.

4. Fold the paper in half and unfold; fold in half the other way and unfold. Insert your thumbs and index fingers into the four square flaps on one side, and move your fingers back and forth, opening the fortune teller's "mouth" in alternating directions. To go with the New Year's Day theme, we wrote the names of the months on each of the four flaps and the eight triangles inside the teller, but you can use letters, numbers, colors, or any other words you like. Underneath those eight triangles, write the fortunes (see suggestions, opposite). To tell a fortune, have someone choose one of the months from the first four flaps, then open/close the teller one time for each letter in that month; repeat twice, with months on the inside triangles; have the person choose a month once more. Lift the flap to reveal the fortune beneath.

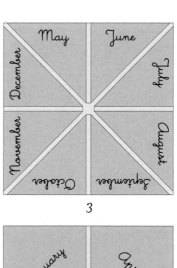

3

4

SEEING THE FUTURE *Use a metallic pen to inscribe the fortune tellers. The fortunes can be answers to questions: "Ask again," "Time will tell," "Not a chance." Or write predictions for the coming year: "A letter will arrive from a secret admirer," "You will find all your long-lost socks," "A rainbow will appear on a cloudless day." You can write in fortunes before guests arrive, or leave them blank and let filling them in be part of the fun.*

part

3

THE RECIPES

SIT DOWN TO
ANY OF OUR FIVE
SUMPTUOUS
FEASTS OR MIX
AND MATCH
RECIPES FOR
AN ALTOGETHER
DIFFERENT
CELEBRATION

MENU

cocktails

Maestro's old-fashioned

wild-mushroom pâté

buffet

oyster pie

chicken hash

over toasted skillet corn bread

citrus salad

baked country ham

with beaten biscuits

marinated green bean

and butter bean salad

dessert

Nana's Japanese fruitcake

Grandmother Miller's

pecan rolls

Salli's cranberry tartlets

steamed persimmon pudding

Freedom Hall beet cake

gingerbread angels

PARTY PLAN

FOUR DAYS BEFORE
Make candied orange zest for cake.
Make gingerbread dough.
Make beaten biscuits.

TWO DAYS BEFORE
Make steamed pudding.
Make pecan-roll dough.
Make beet cake.
Make gingerbread angels.

ONE DAY BEFORE
Make wild-mushroom pâté.
Make fruitcake layers and filling.
Glaze beet cake.
Make corn bread and chicken hash.

NIGHT BEFORE
Cook ham.

MORNING OF PARTY
Bake pecan rolls.
Make cranberry pies.
Assemble fruitcake.

JUST BEFORE
Unmold pâté, and garnish.
Bake oyster pie.
Section fruit.
Warm biscuits, hash, and steamed pudding.
Toast corn bread.
Prepare all salads.
Mix up the cocktails.

Maestro's Old-Fashioned

SERVES 1

1   cube of sugar
    Dash angostura bitters
2   ounces very best bourbon
    Orange zest
    Orange slice for garnish

Put the sugar into an old-fashioned glass with bitters and 2 drops cold water; stir a bit to dissolve the sugar. Add ice cubes and bourbon. Stir. Twist the orange zest over the drink to release the oils, then drop in. Garnish with an orange slice. Serve immediately.

Wild-Mushroom Pâté

SERVES 12 TO 24 AS AN APPETIZER

The pâté, which should be chilled for at least eight hours, may be made up to one day ahead. Serve with toast points made from thin-sliced white sandwich bread; remove crusts, and toast just until golden.

1   cup walnuts, finely chopped, plus
    more for garnish
6   tablespoons unsalted butter
2½ pounds assorted mushrooms, such as
    cremini, shiitake, portobello, and white
    button, cleaned and chopped into
    medium pieces, plus 14 to 16 small
    mushrooms, halved for garnish
6   scallions, white and pale-green parts,
    finely chopped
1½ tablespoons fresh thyme leaves
    (see the Guide), finely chopped,
    plus more for garnish
1½ teaspoons salt, plus more to taste
1   teaspoon freshly ground pepper,
    plus more to taste
⅓   cup dry sherry
    Juice of 1 lemon
1   cup flat-leaf parsley leaves,
    finely chopped
    Dash Tabasco sauce
1   eight-ounce package cream cheese,
    room temperature

1. Heat oven to 350°. Spread walnuts on a baking pan. Bake until fragrant, about 7 minutes. Transfer walnuts to a bowl; set aside to cool.
2. In a large heavy skillet over medium heat, melt 4 tablespoons of butter, and cook the chopped mushrooms and scallions, stirring occasionally, until liquid has been released and the skillet becomes almost dry, about 20 minutes. Stir in thyme, salt, and pepper; cook 2 more minutes. Add sherry, and cook until skillet is almost dry, 4 minutes. Stir in lemon juice. Remove from heat, and let cool.
3. In a large bowl, combine the mushroom mixture with the reserved toasted walnuts, parsley, Tabasco sauce, and cream cheese. Season with salt and pepper to taste.
4. Line a 12½-by-4-by-3-inch terrine (see the Guide; or use any 6-cup mold) with plastic wrap, allowing for a 4-inch overhang on all sides. Spoon mushroom mixture into terrine. Firmly press down all over terrine with your hands; spread mixture as evenly as possible. Cover mold with the overhanging plastic wrap; chill for at least 8 hours or overnight.
5. Just before serving, melt the remaining 2 tablespoons butter in a medium skillet, and cook the halved mushrooms just until tender, about 5 minutes. Season with salt and pepper. Unwrap the chilled terrine, and invert it onto a large serving platter. Use a warm, wet towel on top of the mold, if necessary, to help loosen the terrine. Garnish the serving platter with the cooked mushroom halves, remaining walnuts, and thyme leaves. Serve with toast points, water biscuits, or any plain cracker.

Oyster Pie

SERVES 10 TO 12

This oyster pie has a simple, quick crust made of crushed cracker crumbs; there's no need to make a piecrust.

14   tablespoons unsalted butter (1¾ sticks),
     plus more for dish
1½   quarts shucked oysters and their liquid
     (see the Guide)
7   scallions, white and pale-green parts,
     finely chopped
1   teaspoon Worcestershire sauce
¾   teaspoon Tabasco sauce
1   cup chopped fresh flat-leaf parsley
1   teaspoon salt
¼   teaspoon freshly ground pepper
3   cups saltine cracker crumbs, crumbled
     by hand, made from about 46 crackers
3   tablespoons half-and-half or milk

1. Butter a shallow 9- to 10-inch baking or pie dish. Heat oven to 450° with rack in center. Reserving liquid, drain the oysters. Check oysters for shells, and discard. Melt 3 tablespoons butter over medium heat in a medium skillet, and cook scallions until soft, 3 minutes. Stir in Worcestershire sauce and Tabasco sauce. Transfer mixture to a medium bowl; let cool.
2. Stir in oysters, ¼ cup parsley, salt, and pepper. In a medium bowl, combine cracker crumbs and remaining ¾ cup parsley. Melt remaining 11 tablespoons butter, and stir into crumb mixture. In a small bowl, combine ¼ cup of the reserved oyster liquid with the half-and-half. Spread an even, thin layer of the crumb mixture in the bottom of the baking dish. Cover with one-third of the oyster mixture. Cover with ½ cup crumb mixture, followed by one-third of the oyster liquid. Continue until all ingredients are used, two more times, ending with crumb mixture. Bake until golden brown on top, 25 to 35 minutes. Serve hot.

Chicken Hash Over Toasted Skillet Corn Bread

SERVES 10 TO 12

Salli likes to use local hickory-smoked bacon for her hash.

- 1 five-pound chicken
- 1 stalk celery
- 3 sprigs fresh thyme (see the Guide)
- 6 sprigs fresh flat-leaf parsley
- 10 whole black peppercorns
- 1 onion, quartered
- 2 dried bay leaves
- 1 pound thick-cut sliced bacon
- 6 tablespoons unsalted butter
- 3 cloves garlic, minced
- 1 large onion, medium chopped
- 2 red bell peppers, seeds and ribs removed, cut into 2-inch strips
- 2 yellow bell peppers, seeds and ribs removed, cut into 2-inch strips
  Salt and freshly ground pepper
- 3/4 pound white button mushrooms, cleaned, thinly sliced
- 1/2 cup dry white wine
- 2 tablespoons chopped fresh rosemary, plus more for garnish
- 2 tablespoons cornstarch
  Juice of 1 lemon
- 1 recipe Skillet Corn Bread (recipe follows)

1. In a stockpot place the chicken, celery, thyme, parsley, peppercorns, quartered onion, and 1 dried bay leaf. Fill with water to cover chicken. Cover, and bring to a boil over high heat. Reduce to a simmer; cook until chicken is cooked through, about 1 hour. Strain. Remove chicken, and allow to cool. Discard solids from stock mixture, and set stock aside (you will need about 4 cups of the stock). Once chicken cools, remove and discard skin. Cut meat into roughly 1/2- to 1/4-inch pieces. Set aside.
2. In a large skillet, cook bacon until crisp. Reserving 3 tablespoons bacon grease, set aside bacon to cool; crumble bacon, and set aside. Add 2 tablespoons butter to bacon grease in skillet; cook over medium heat until melted. Add garlic, onion, and red and yellow bell peppers. Season with salt and pepper. Cook until soft and translucent, 10 minutes. Add mushrooms, and cook, stirring occasionally, until soft, about

5 minutes. Taste for seasoning. Stir in 3 cups reserved chicken stock and the wine. Add remaining bay leaf and rosemary, and cook hash for 10 to 15 minutes.
3. Stir the cornstarch into 1/2 cup of remaining chicken stock until smooth. Stir cornstarch mixture into hash, and cook 10 minutes. Add reserved chicken; stir to combine. Continue to cook until chicken is heated through. If too thick, add some of the remaining stock. Stir in lemon juice and reserved bacon. Season with salt and pepper, if desired. Heat until hot.
4. Just before serving, cut the corn bread into 12 wedges. Split each wedge in half crosswise. Butter each half with remaining butter. Transfer to a baking sheet, and toast, butter-side up, under a broiler until golden brown. Serve the hot chicken hash over warm corn bread wedges, garnished with rosemary.

Skillet Corn Bread

SERVES 8 TO 12

If you plan to serve a larger crowd, and have two heavy skillets, two batches of this recipe can be baked at once.

- 1/4 cup pure vegetable shortening
- 2 cups all-purpose flour
- 2 cups white or yellow cornmeal
- 2 teaspoons sugar
- 4 teaspoons salt
- 4 teaspoons baking powder
- 2 cups milk
- 4 large eggs

1. Heat oven to 425° with rack in center of oven. Place shortening in a 10-inch cast-iron skillet. Place in oven.
2. In a medium bowl, whisk together flour, cornmeal, sugar, salt, and baking powder. Set aside. In a small bowl, whisk together milk and eggs until frothy. Pour milk mixture into reserved dry ingredients. Mix just until ingredients are incorporated. Do not overmix; batter should be lumpy. Carefully remove hot skillet from oven. Pour batter into it; return to oven. Cook until top is golden and a skewer inserted in center comes out dry; 25 to 35 minutes.

Citrus Salad

SERVES 10 TO 12

The most beautiful ruby-red grapefruit is available in December; use it to make this jewel-like salad. In other seasons the grapefruit will be smaller and you will need more.

- 4 ruby-red or pink grapefruit, peel and pith removed
- 5 navel or blood oranges, peel and pith removed
- 3 tablespoons sherry vinegar
  Salt and freshly ground pepper
- 1 tablespoon honey
- 5 tablespoons extra-virgin olive oil
- 1/4 cup canola oil
- 2 large heads radicchio, leaves separated
- 2 heads Belgian endive, leaves separated
- 1/4 small red onion, very thinly sliced

1. Working over a bowl to catch the juices, use a paring knife to slice between sections and membranes of each grapefruit; remove segments whole. Place each segment in bowl. Repeat with oranges. Add to bowl. Transfer to refrigerator while proceeding. Recipe may be made up to this point 1 hour ahead.
2. In a small bowl, combine vinegar, salt and pepper to taste, and the honey. Slowly whisk in olive oil, then the canola oil, until mixture is well combined. Set vinaigrette aside.
3. Just before serving, arrange radicchio and endive leaves on a large serving platter. Arrange grapefruit and orange segments in center of platter. Scatter red onion over top. Drizzle vinaigrette over the salad, and serve.

Baked Country Ham

SERVES 36 TO 60

Prepare this ham the night before serving. The ham should be cut into very thin slivers; it is quite salty and is best eaten in small quantities.

- *1 sixteen-pound country-cured ham (see the Guide)*

1. Soak ham in a large kettle or pot, or fill up your sink with water and soak it there. Soak ham for 4 to 8 hours to lose some of the saltiness; change water two or three times if possible. Rinse well; scrape off any mold or green rind.
2. Wrap ham in aluminum foil. Place on a baking sheet. At 7 p.m. the night before you plan to serve the ham, heat oven to 500°. Place wrapped ham in a large roasting pan, filled with 1 inch of water; bake for 30 minutes. Turn off oven, but do not open door. At 10 p.m. turn oven back on to 500°. Bake ham for another 15 minutes. Turn off oven, but do not open door. Leave ham in closed oven overnight.
3. Remove ham from oven; remove foil. Using a very sharp knife, trim rind and all the fat from the ham. Serve ham warm or at room temperature; cut with a ham-slicing knife into very thin slivers. Serve with beaten biscuits.

Beaten Biscuits

MAKES 3 DOZEN

These are more like soda crackers than flaky doughy biscuits; they are small and firm. For best results, bake them in the oven one sheet at a time.

- *1 cup plus ¾ cup all-purpose flour, plus more for work surface and rolling out dough*
- *2 teaspoons salt*
- *3 tablespoons unsalted butter, cut into small pieces*
- *¼ cup pure vegetable shortening*
- *¼ cup milk*

1. Line two baking sheets with dull side of aluminum foil facing up. Set aside. In bowl of a food processor, pulse to combine flour and salt. Add butter and shortening; pulse until mixture resembles fine meal. With machine running, pour in milk and ¼ cup ice water through feed tube. Mix until most of dough has formed a ball; continue for 2 minutes.
2. Heat oven to 300° with rack in center. Transfer the dough to a lightly floured surface. The dough will appear wet and slick. Sprinkle top of dough lightly with flour. Use a rolling pin to beat across the top of the dough, beating in the flour, until the dough is about 10 inches long and ½-inch thick. Fold up the dough loosely into thirds, sprinkle again with flour, and beat flour in. Stretch out dough again until it is about ¼-inch thick. Sprinkle the dough again with flour, and repeat process for about 10 minutes. The dough will become very smooth, and little bubbles will form in it. As the dough is beaten with the flour and folded, very thin layers form in the dough.
3. When the dough is smooth and satiny, roll out until ⅜-inch thick. Cut out biscuit rounds with a 1½-inch biscuit cutter. Transfer the rounds to prepared baking sheets, placing them about 1 inch apart. Prick each round twice with the tines of a small fork, poking fork all the way down through the dough to the baking sheet.
4. One sheet at a time, bake biscuits 15 minutes; reduce heat to 200°. Continue to bake until biscuits are golden brown on bottom but not colored on top; biscuits will dry out in center as well. Watch carefully; this can take anywhere from 15 to 30 minutes more. The biscuits actually turn a very slight white-pink color when done; they should not be golden or brown on top at all. Continue to sprinkle any remaining dough with flour; beat and bake any scraps of dough until all dough has been used. Serve biscuits cut in half with very thin slivers of baked country ham. Biscuits freeze well in an airtight container, up to 1 month.

Marinated Green Bean and Butter Bean Salad

SERVES 10

Butter beans, or small lima beans, are fresh in the summer. You can freeze them to use all winter, but frozen small limas may be used as well. Any extra vinaigrette can be stored in an airtight container and refrigerated for another use. Fresh butter beans will cook for 25 to 30 minutes—much longer than frozen lima beans.

- *2 pounds fresh green beans, ends snapped*
  Salt
- *1 pound 4 ounces butter beans, or small fresh or frozen lima beans*
- *¼ cup tarragon or white wine vinegar*
- *3 tablespoons Dijon mustard*
  Freshly ground pepper
- *1 minced shallot*
- *¾ cup extra-virgin olive oil*
- *2 tablespoons chopped fresh tarragon (see the Guide), plus more for garnish*
- *2 tablespoons chopped fresh flat-leaf parsley, plus more for garnish*

1. Cook green beans in boiling, salted water, just until bright green and tender, about 5 minutes. Reserving cooking liquid, remove beans with a large slotted spoon; transfer to a large bowl of ice water to stop cooking. Transfer beans to a colander. Cook butter beans in the boiling cooking liquid, just until tender, 5 minutes if frozen. Strain; place under cold, running water to stop cooking. Set aside.
2. In a medium bowl, combine vinegar, mustard, salt and pepper to taste, and minced shallot. Whisk in the olive oil until vinaigrette is creamy. Whisk in tarragon and parsley.
3. In a large bowl, toss the green beans until well coated with about three-quarters of the vinaigrette. In a large bowl or on a platter, arrange green beans in an even layer. Sprinkle butter beans over the top. Drizzle remaining vinaigrette over beans. Garnish with tarragon and parsley. Serve at room temperature.

Nana's Japanese Fruitcake

SERVES 10 TO 12

This cake is not a traditional fruitcake but a delicious three-layer spice cake. Use three eight-by-two-inch-deep cake pans to make each layer; the filling may be made a day ahead.

FOR THE CAKE:

- 2   cups walnuts, finely chopped
      Unsalted butter for pans and parchment
- 3   cups all-purpose flour
- 1   tablespoon baking powder
- 1   teaspoon baking soda
- 1   teaspoon salt
- 1/2 cup golden raisins
- 1 1/2 teaspoons ground cinnamon
- 1 1/2 teaspoons allspice
- 2 1/2 cups sugar
- 1   cup pure vegetable shortening
- 4   large eggs
- 1 1/2 cups milk

FOR THE FILLING:

- 1   pineapple, peeled, cored, finely chopped to equal one pound
- 4   navel oranges, peel and pith removed, segmented
- 2   coconuts, grated, or 3 cups unsweetened flaked coconut
- 1 1/2 cups sugar
- 1/4 cup plus 2 tablespoons cornstarch
- 1   recipe Seven-Minute Frosting (recipe follows)
- 1   recipe Candied Orange Zest (recipe follows)

1. FOR THE CAKE: Heat oven to 350° with racks placed in center. Spread nuts on a baking pan. Bake until fragrant, about 7 minutes. Transfer nuts to a bowl; set aside to cool.

2. Line bottoms of three 8-by-2-inch buttered cake pans with parchment paper; butter the parchment. Dust bottoms and sides of pan with flour; tap out any excess. In a large bowl, whisk together flour, baking powder, baking soda, and salt. Set aside. Finely chop raisins; combine with cinnamon and allspice. Set aside.

3. With an electric mixer fitted with paddle attachment, beat together sugar and shortening on medium speed until combined. Add eggs one at a time, beating well after each addition. On low speed, add flour mixture and milk to batter, alternating between the two, starting and ending with dry ingredients.

4. Fold raisin mixture into one-third of the batter. Pour batter into one cake pan. Stir reserved toasted walnuts into remaining batter. Divide batter between two remaining cake pans. Bake, rotating pans for even baking if necessary, until a cake tester inserted in middle comes out clean, about 40 minutes. Transfer to cooling racks to cool; invert cakes onto cooling rack. Allow to cool completely.

5. FOR THE FILLING: Combine pineapple, oranges, 2 cups coconut, and sugar in a medium saucepan. Bring to a boil over high heat, stirring. Reduce to a simmer; let cook, stirring, until thickened, about 20 minutes. Whisk cornstarch into 1/4 cup warm water. Stir into filling. Continue to cook until thick, 6 minutes. Let cool before using.

6. Place one walnut layer top-side down on serving plate. Top with half of filling. Place raisin layer, top-side up, securely on top; press down lightly. Using offset spatula, go around layers to press filling between layers. Top with remaining filling. Place remaining walnut layer on top, top-side up. Press down with hands. Using offset spatula, go around layers again to ensure filling is securely between layers. Frost sides of cake first, using an offset spatula. Ice top of cake; decorate with drained candied orange zest and remaining coconut. Serve.

Seven-Minute Frosting

MAKES ENOUGH FOR 1 CAKE

- 3/4 cup plus 2 tablespoons sugar
- 1   tablespoon light corn syrup
- 3   large egg whites

1. In a small heavy saucepan, combine 3/4 cup sugar, corn syrup, and 1/3 cup water. Heat over medium heat, stirring until sugar has dissolved. Increase heat to bring to a boil. Do not stir anymore. Boil, washing down sides of pan with a wet pastry brush to prevent crystals from forming, until a candy thermometer (see the Guide) registers 230°, about 7 minutes.

2. Meanwhile, whisk egg whites in an electric mixer fitted with paddle attachment until soft peaks form, about 2 1/2 minutes on medium speed. Gradually add remaining 2 tablespoons sugar. Remove syrup from heat when temperature reaches 230°; it will keep rising as pan is removed from heat. At no higher than 235°, pour syrup in a steady stream down side of bowl containing egg-white mixture, with mixer on medium-low speed.

3. Beat frosting on medium speed until it is cool, about 9 minutes. Frosting should be thick and shiny. Use immediately to frost cake.

Candied Orange Zest

MAKES 1 CUP

The candied zest will keep in an airtight container in the refrigerator for up to one month; it may be used to decorate all kinds of holiday desserts.

- 4   oranges, scrubbed
- 1   cup sugar

1. Using a vegetable peeler, peel zest from oranges. Use a knife to remove any white pith; cut zest as thinly as possible into strips.

2. Bring 1 cup water to a boil in a medium saucepan. Add zest; blanch for 1 minute, drain, and rinse under cold water.

3. In another medium saucepan, combine sugar and 1 cup water; bring to a simmer. Cook until sugar dissolves completely; about 2 minutes. Add zest. Simmer until translucent, about 30 minutes. Remove from heat; let zest cool in syrup. When cool, transfer zest and syrup to an airtight plastic container.

Grandmother Miller's Pecan Rolls

MAKES ABOUT 6 DOZEN

This recipe may be halved for fewer pecan rolls.

FOR THE PASTRY:

- 4 cups all-purpose flour, plus more for work surface
- 1 teaspoon salt
- 2/3 cup pure vegetable shortening, cut into small pieces
- 11 tablespoons unsalted butter, cut into small pieces

FOR THE FILLING:

- 1 cup chopped pecans, about 4 ounces
- 1/2 cup packed dark-brown sugar
- 1/2 cup granulated sugar
- 2 large eggs, lightly beaten
- 6 teaspoons unsalted butter
- 2 tablespoons milk
- 2 tablespoons heavy cream
- 1/2 teaspoon pure vanilla extract

FOR THE GLAZE:

- 1 large egg
- 1 tablespoon heavy cream
- 5 teaspoons granulated sugar

1. FOR THE PASTRY: Whisk together flour and salt in a medium bowl. Using a pastry cutter or two forks, work in shortening, until mixture resembles coarse meal. Stirring with a fork, pour in 2/3 cup ice water, or more as needed, just until mixture holds together; do not overmix. Roll out dough on a lightly floured surface into an approximate 15-by-20-inch piece. Dot dough with one-third of the butter. Fold dough in half, lengthwise, then into thirds, like a letter (fold one-third up from bottom, then fold top third over bottom third). Wrap in plastic wrap; refrigerate until chilled, 30 minutes to 1 hour. Remove and repeat process of rolling out dough and dotting with butter, twice more, until all butter is used, chilling each time. Wrap and return to refrigerator until ready to use. Dough may be made up to 2 days ahead.

2. Heat oven to 350°. Spread pecans on a baking pan. Bake until fragrant, about 7 minutes. Transfer pecans to a bowl; set aside to cool.

3. FOR THE FILLING: Place brown sugar, granulated sugar, toasted pecans, eggs, butter, milk, cream, and vanilla in a large, heavy skillet. Cook over medium heat, stirring often as ingredients melt, until mixture begins to thicken, about 5 minutes. Reduce heat to low, and continue to cook, stirring occasionally, until mixture thickens, about 5 minutes more.

4. Increase oven heat to 400° with rack in center. Cut dough in half, wrap half in plastic, and refrigerate until ready to roll and bake.

5. On a lightly floured surface, roll out half the dough to a 1/8-inch thickness, and, using a 1 3/4-inch cutter, cut out dough into 70 to 80 rounds. (If dough becomes too soft, place on a cookie sheet and chill for about 20 minutes.) Roll out remaining dough, cut out 80 1 3/4-inch circles, and then use a 1-inch cookie cutter to cut out centers of these circles. Fill each whole circle with 1/2 teaspoon pecan filling. Top each with cut-out rounds, with centers exposed. Transfer filled pecan rolls to baking sheets.

6. FOR THE GLAZE: In a small bowl, combine egg and heavy cream. Lightly brush pecan rolls with glaze. Sprinkle each with sugar. Bake until golden and flaky, 10 to 12 minutes. Serve warm or at room temperature. Pecan rolls are best eaten within a day of being made.

Salli's Cranberry Tartlets

MAKES 15

You will need 3-by-3/4-inch round, tartlet molds with removable bottoms (see the Guide). You may work in batches with fewer pans.

- 3/4 cup roughly chopped walnuts, plus 5 tablespoons for sprinkling
- 12 tablespoons (1 1/2 sticks) unsalted butter, melted, plus more melted for pans
- 3/4 cup sugar
- 2 large eggs, lightly beaten
- 1 teaspoon pure almond extract
- 1 cup all-purpose flour
- 2 cups fresh or frozen cranberries
- 1/4 teaspoon amber or crystal sugar for sprinkling (optional; see the Guide)

1. Heat oven to 350° with rack in center. Spread nuts on a baking pan. Bake until fragrant, about 7 minutes. Transfer nuts to a bowl; set aside to cool.

2. Reduce oven heat to 325°. Brush tartlet pans with melted butter. In a large bowl, whisk together 12 tablespoons melted butter, sugar, eggs, almond extract, and flour. Batter will be thick. Stir in cranberries and nuts.

3. Fill each pan with 1/2 cup batter. Sprinkle each top with 1 teaspoon walnuts and amber sugar. Bake until golden and slightly crusty on top, 30 to 40 minutes. A cake tester inserted in the center should come out clean. Transfer to a cooling rack. Once cool, remove tarts from pans. These are best served within a day.

Steamed Persimmon Pudding

SERVES 8 TO 10

Rewarm pudding in its mold, in 350° oven for about 40 minutes.

- ¾ cup pecans, coarsely chopped
- ¼ cup brandy
- ¼ cup golden raisins
- ¼ cup currants
- 3 tablespoons unsalted butter, softened
- 1 cup sugar
- 2 large eggs, separated
- 1 teaspoon pure vanilla extract
- 2 teaspoons freshly squeezed lemon juice
- 1 teaspoon baking soda
- 1 tablespoon hot water
- 2 to 3 very ripe persimmons
- ¾ cup half-and-half
- 1¼ cups all-purpose flour
- 1½ teaspoons ground cinnamon
- ½ teaspoon ground nutmeg
- ¼ teaspoon salt

1. Heat oven to 350°. Spread pecans on a baking pan. Bake until fragrant, about 7 minutes. Transfer pecans to a bowl; set aside to cool.

2. Butter an 8-cup lidded pudding mold, and set aside. In a small saucepan over low heat, combine brandy, raisins, and currants, and bring to a simmer. Remove from heat, and let sit for 15 minutes.

3. Meanwhile, in the bowl of an electric mixer, cream butter and sugar. Beat in egg yolks, vanilla, and lemon juice. Dissolve baking soda in hot water; add to egg mixture. Set aside.

4. Cut tops off persimmons. Scoop out pulp and push through a strainer, discarding seeds and skins. Combine persimmon pulp with half-and-half in a large bowl. Set aside.

5. Sift together flour, spices, and salt, and add to persimmon mixture. Gradually beat persimmon-flour mixture into egg mixture. Stir in pecans and reserved raisin-currant mixture. Set aside. In a clean bowl, beat egg whites until stiff peaks form; fold into batter. Pour batter into mold, and tap down lightly to remove any air bubbles; clamp on lid.

6. Choose a pot large enough to hold mold with a 2-inch clearance on all sides. Place a wire rack or folded dish towel in bottom of pan, and fill with enough water to reach halfway up sides of mold. Cover and bring to a boil; reduce to a simmer. Place mold on rack in pot. Cover and steam pudding for 2 hours 20 minutes. Add boiling water as necessary to maintain water level. Remove mold from pot and let cool, uncovered, for 15 minutes before serving.

Freedom Hall Beet Cake

SERVES 12 TO 15

The secret to this super-moist chocolate cake is cooked beets. Decorate with Gingerbread Angels.

FOR THE CAKE:

- 3 pounds beets
- 3½ cups all-purpose flour
- 4 teaspoons baking soda
- ½ teaspoon salt
- ¼ teaspoon ground cloves
- ¼ teaspoon ground cinnamon
- 5 ounces unsweetened chocolate, chopped
- 6 large eggs
- 2½ cups granulated sugar
- ¼ cup packed dark-brown sugar
- 1½ cups vegetable oil
- 1½ teaspoons pure vanilla extract

FOR THE GLAZE:

- 6 ounces semisweet or good-quality bitter-sweet chocolate (see the Guide), chopped
- 1 tablespoon unsalted butter
- 1 tablespoon light corn syrup
- ¾ cup heavy cream
- Pinch of salt
- ¼ teaspoon ground cinnamon
- ½ teaspoon pure vanilla extract

1. FOR THE CAKE: Wash and trim beets to within an inch of beet. Place in a saucepan of cold water; bring to a boil over high heat. Reduce to a simmer; cook until very tender when pierced with tip of knife, about 1 hour. Drain; let rest until cool enough to handle. Rub off peel with fingers, paper towels, or an old kitchen towel. Cut beets into large pieces; transfer to bowl of a food processor. Process until smooth, 5 minutes. Set aside 4 cups beet purée.

2. In a large bowl, whisk together flour, baking soda, salt, cloves, and cinnamon; set aside. In top of double boiler placed over 1 inch of simmering water, melt chocolate. Let cool.

3. Heat oven to 350° with rack in lower third. With electric mixer fitted with whisk attachment, beat eggs and granulated sugar on medium-low speed until combined. Beat in brown sugar until combined. Beat in vegetable oil. On low speed, gradually beat in beet purée. Add dry ingredients, alternating with melted chocolate. Add vanilla; beat until combined. Pour batter into 12-cup tube pan (see the Guide). Bake until cake tester inserted in middle comes out clean, about 1 hour 35 minutes. Transfer to cooling rack to cool. Invert pan; remove cake. If necessary, trim top to ensure cake will sit evenly on plate. Cake will keep for 2 to 3 days at room temperature, wrapped in plastic wrap.

4. FOR THE GLAZE: When ready to serve, melt chocolate in top of a double boiler placed over 1 inch of simmering water. Add the butter, corn syrup, and cream; stir until smooth. Stir in salt, cinnamon, and vanilla. Pour glaze over cake; use a spatula if necessary to push glaze over sides of cake. Serve at room temperature.

Gingerbread Angels

MAKES 10 DOZEN

This dough freezes beautifully; bake just half the batch if you like.

- 3½ cups all-purpose flour
- 2 teaspoons baking soda
- 1 teaspoon ground cinnamon
- 1 teaspoon ground ginger
- 1 teaspoon ground cloves
- 1 teaspoon allspice
- ¼ teaspoon salt
- 1 cup (2 sticks) unsalted butter, softened
- ¾ cup granulated sugar
- ¾ cup packed dark-brown sugar
- 1 large egg
- 2 tablespoons light corn syrup
   Grated zest of 1 orange
   Grated zest of 1 lemon
- 1 recipe Royal Icing (recipe, page 125)

1. In a medium bowl, combine the flour, baking soda, cinnamon, ginger, cloves, allspice, and salt. Whisk to combine.
2. In the bowl of an electric mixer, beat the butter for 30 seconds, add the granulated sugar and dark-brown sugar, and beat until fluffy. Add egg and corn syrup. Mix well.
3. Add half the dry ingredients to butter mixture; mix until well combined. Add remaining dry ingredients and orange and lemon zests; continue mixing until well combined.
4. Cover and chill the dough about 1 hour, until firm.
5. Heat oven to 350°. On a lightly floured surface, roll out dough to ¼-inch thick, cut out shapes, and place on an ungreased cooked sheet ¾ inch apart; bake 6 to 8 minutes. Transfer to a cooling rack; let cool. Gather scraps into a ball, cover with plastic, and re-chill for 30 minutes. Roll out again to a ¼-inch thick, and cut out additional angels until all the dough is used. Bake cookies.
6. To ice cookies, fill a piping bag fitted with a small round tip, such as #3, with the icing. Pipe 2 small eyes and a smiling mouth onto each angel. Cookies may be made up to 3 days ahead.

How to Decorate Cookies

Working With a Template

Trace the templates on page 68 onto a piece of heavy plastic (a plastic cover from a ring binder works well) or heavy cardboard. Plastic templates are particularly useful, because they may be cleaned and reused. Cut templates out. Roll out dough, and place templates as close together as possible. Use a paring knife to carefully cut around templates and through the cookie dough. Transfer the cookies to a cookie sheet, and as bake as in recipe (at left).

Flooding With Royal Icing

Royal icing (recipe, page 125) is white. You may use any food coloring or gel colors to color icing before it is used. Fill piping bags, fitted with small round tips, such as #2, #3, and #4, with colored icings. Keep icings, tip-ends down, in water glasses with a damp paper towel in bottom of each; this keeps the icing from drying out. Work on one cookie at a time; pipe an outline around the edge for a border. Fill the inside roughly with icing squiggles.

Spreading

Use a small offset spatula to evenly spread out the icing inside the border for a smooth, flooded surface. This surface may now be decorated.

Flocking

Flocking is the process in which sanding sugar (see the Guide) is sprinkled onto wet icing so that it sticks and makes a frosty-looking decoration. Use a small spoon to sprinkle the sugar evenly over the wet icing. Any excess sugar may be tapped off and reused.

MENU

lunch Christmas **sandwiches**
macaroni and **cheese**
piglets in blankets
chocolate-bar hot chocolate

PARTY PLAN

ONE DAY BEFORE
Grate cheese for macaroni.

MORNING OF PARTY
Chop chocolate.
Wrap mini hot dogs in dough.
Parboil pasta.
Prepare ramekins of macaroni.

TWO HOURS BEFORE
Prepare sandwiches.

JUST BEFORE
Bake macaroni and cheese.
Warm hot chocolate.
Transfer sandwiches to platters.
Bake piglets in blankets.

Christmas Sandwiches

Reserve the cut-out sections of the bread, and make cinnamon toast with them to serve with the hot chocolate; spread each with a slick of butter, sprinkle with sugar and ground cinnamon, and toast until golden.

- 1 large loaf presliced whole-wheat sandwich bread (18 slices)
- 1 large loaf presliced white sandwich bread (18 slices)
- 1 eighteen-ounce jar creamy peanut butter
- 1 twelve-ounce jar orange or strawberry jam or jelly

1. Trim the crusts off the bread, working with two slices at a time, so each sandwich will look neat and uniform.
2. Using a cookie cutter no larger than 2½ inches (so the cutter will fit the bread slices), cut out the design on one slice of bread from each sandwich pair.
3. On the second slice of bread from each pair, spread the peanut butter in an even layer. Spread a thin layer of jam over peanut butter.
4. Cover each bottom with its decorative top to create a window-pane effect. Sandwiches may be made up to 2 hours ahead and covered with a slightly dampened paper towel to keep them moist, or they may be placed on a tray and tightly wrapped with plastic wrap until ready to serve.

Macaroni and Cheese

Making macaroni and cheese in individual ramekins makes each child feel special; curly noodles add a festive touch.

- 6 tablespoons unsalted butter, plus more for ramekins
  Salt
- 1 pound corkscrew pasta (cavatappi)
- 5½ cups milk
- ½ cup all-purpose flour
- ¼ teaspoon freshly ground pepper
- 3¼ cups grated white cheddar cheese (from 10 ounces)
- 3¼ cups grated orange cheddar cheese (from 10 ounces)

1. Heat oven to 375°. Lightly butter the ramekins; set aside.
2. Fill a large saucepan with salted water, cover and bring to a boil. Add pasta; cook 2 to 3 minutes less than instructions on package, until outside of pasta is cooked and the inside is underdone. (Different brands of pasta cook at different rates; be sure to read instructions.)
3. Transfer pasta to a colander; rinse under cold running water, and drain well. Set aside.
4. In a medium saucepan placed over medium heat, heat the milk until very hot, but do not boil or scorch.
5. In a high-sided skillet, melt 6 tablespoons of butter over medium heat. When butter bubbles, stir in flour. Cook, whisking constantly for approximately 1 minute. While still whisking, slowly pour in hot milk. Continue cooking and whisking constantly, until mixture bubbles and becomes thick, 7 to 10 minutes.
6. Remove the pan from heat. Stir in 2 teaspoons salt, the pepper, and 2¼ cups of each of the cheddar cheeses.
7. Add drained pasta into the cheese sauce, and stir until all of the pasta is covered. Stir gently to avoid breaking the noodles.
8. Spoon macaroni and cheese into prepared ramekins. Ramekins may be prepared up to this point, covered with plastic wrap, and refrigerated up to 4 hours. Sprinkle top of each ramekin with remaining cheeses. Transfer ramekins to a baking pan; bake until golden brown on top, about 25 minutes. Serve hot.

Piglets in Blankets

This recipe uses the traditional crescent-roll dough found in the refrigerated section of the grocery store, and miniature hot dogs; look for kosher miniature hot dogs or sausages.

- 1 eight-ounce package crescent-roll dough
- 2 ten-ounce packages miniature hot dogs
- 1 large egg

1. Heat oven to 375°. Unroll dough onto a work surface. Use a sharp knife to cut out 4-by-⅛-inch strips. Wrap one strip of dough tightly around each hot dog to create a spiral effect. (Hot dogs may be wrapped in other ways with the dough if you wish.) Hot dogs may be made up to this stage, arranged on a baking pan, covered with plastic wrap, and refrigerated for up to 8 hours.
2. Just before baking, whisk the egg with 2 teaspoons of water in a small bowl for an egg wash. Using a pastry brush, brush the dough with the egg wash before baking. Bake until golden brown, 10 to 15 minutes. Serve hot.

Chocolate-Bar Hot Chocolate

Hot chocolate made from candy bars is a child's idea of heaven. Actually, it just saves time because the sugar is already added. Candy-cane stirrers give the chocolate a hint of peppermint flavor.

- 1 eight-ounce Hershey's chocolate bar, finely chopped
- 1 quart milk
- 4 candy canes, for swizzle sticks

Combine the chocolate and milk in a medium saucepan. Heat over medium heat, whisking often until chocolate has melted, about 5 minutes. Whisk the mixture to combine well. Serve hot with one candy cane in each mug.

MENU

hors d'oeuvres
finnan-haddie canapés

shrimp-salad rolls

endive petals
with smoked scallops

dinner
creamy red and green cabbage

twice-baked potatoes with
spinach and parsnip soufflés

lobster Newburg

wild-rice dressing

warm string-bean salad

crown roast

dessert
lardy cake

Torie's chocolate-chunk
toffee cookies

chocolate-applesauce cake

PARTY PLAN

ONE WEEK BEFORE
Make finnan-haddie mixture.
*Make chocolate-toffee
cookies.*

ONE DAY BEFORE
Make lobster stock.
Prepare beets for endive petals.
Make lardy cake.
Make wild-rice dressing.

MORNING OF PARTY
Make shrimp salad.
Make lobster Newburg.

THREE HOURS BEFORE
Put crown roast in oven.

JUST BEFORE
*Assemble shrimp rolls,
finnan-haddie, and
endive petals.*
*Bake lobster Newburg and
twice-baked potatoes.*
*Cook cabbage and
string-bean salad.*
Heat dressing.

Finnan-Haddie Canapés

SERVES 6

Smoked haddock, known as finnan haddie after the Scottish village Findon, is available in some fish markets. Salt cod makes a good substitute and is generally easier to find.

- ¼ pound smoked haddock or salt cod
- 1 quart milk
- 1 clove garlic, peeled
- 6 sprigs fresh thyme, plus more for garnish
- 1 small potato, peeled and quartered
- 2 tablespoons heavy cream
- ½ teaspoon salt
- ¼ teaspoon freshly ground black pepper
- 3 tablespoons freshly grated horseradish, or to taste
- 1 twelve-inch-long baguette, sliced into ¼-inch-thick slices on the diagonal
- 1 tablespoon olive oil

1. Place the smoked haddock in a large bowl, and cover with cold water. Soak fish 4 hours, changing water every 30 minutes. Alternatively, keep bowl under a thin stream of constantly running water. If using salt cod, soak the fish 12 hours.
2. Remove haddock from water; discard any bones. Transfer fish to a saucepan. Add milk, garlic, thyme, and potato. Set over medium-low heat; simmer until haddock is very soft, about 1 hour. Pour mixture through a sieve set over a bowl; discard thyme and milk. Transfer solids to a large bowl.
3. Heat oven to 400°. Using a fork, gently mash haddock, potato, and garlic together, adding enough cream to make a thick paste. Add salt and pepper; stir in the horseradish.
4. Place the bread slices on a baking sheet, and toast until golden. Brush toast with olive oil, and spread fish paste on top. Garnish servings with the fresh thyme.

Shrimp-Salad Rolls

SERVES 6

Look for the smallest, sweetest shrimp available. Parker House rolls became famous in the late nineteenth century at Boston's Parker House hotel.

- 1 pound small shrimp, peeled and deveined
- 1 tablespoon unsalted butter
  Salt
  Freshly ground pepper
- 3 tablespoons freshly squeezed lemon juice, plus more to taste
- ¾ cup mayonnaise
- 1 scallion, finely chopped
- 24 Parker House or other small rolls
- 1 small head Bibb lettuce, washed and trimmed

1. Rinse shrimp under cold running water, and pat dry. Heat butter in a large skillet set over medium heat. Add shrimp; season with salt and pepper. Cook shrimp until bright pink and opaque, about 2 minutes per side. Add lemon juice; remove from heat.
2. Let shrimp cool. Cut into ½-inch pieces. In large bowl, combine shrimp, mayonnaise, and scallion; toss to coat. Season shrimp salad with salt, pepper, and lemon juice, if desired. Chill.
3. Split open the rolls. Gently press a lettuce leaf into each roll, and fill with a heaping teaspoon of shrimp salad. Serve.

Endive Petals With Smoked Scallops

SERVES 6

- 2 small red beets
- ½ pound smoked sea scallops (see the Guide), cut into ¼-inch dice
- ½ cup coarsely chopped flat-leaf parsley
- 1 tablespoon freshly squeezed lemon juice
- 2 tablespoons olive oil
- ½ teaspoon salt
- ¼ teaspoon freshly ground pepper
- 2 heads Belgian endive

1. Fill a small saucepan with water. Add beets, and bring to a boil. Reduce heat; simmer until fork tender, about 45 minutes. Remove pan from heat. Drain, peel, and set beets aside to cool. Chop beets into ¼-inch dice.
2. Combine beets, scallops, and parsley in a small bowl. Add lemon juice, olive oil, salt, and pepper. Toss to combine. Serve scallops on individual endive leaves.

Creamy Red and Green Cabbage

SERVES 6

- 1 small head red cabbage
- 1 small head green cabbage
  Salt
- 4 tablespoons unsalted butter
- 1 shallot, peeled and minced
- 1½ teaspoons celery seeds
- 1 cup heavy cream
  Freshly ground pepper

1. Trim both red and green cabbages, discarding tough outer leaves and core. Slice into ¼-inch-thick slices. Bring a large stockpot of water to a boil; add 2 teaspoons salt. Cook red cabbage 1 minute. Using a slotted spoon, transfer cabbage to a colander; drain. Repeat with green cabbage. Pat cabbage dry; set aside.
2. Melt butter in a large skillet set over medium heat. Add shallot and celery seeds; cook until fragrant, about 2 minutes. Add cream; bring to a boil. Reduce heat; simmer until cream has slightly thickened, about 5 minutes.
3. Add cabbage to skillet; season with salt and pepper. Cook cabbage until heated through, 3 to 5 minutes. Serve immediately.

Twice-Baked Potatoes With Spinach and Parsnip Soufflés

SERVES 6

Use the extra potato flesh for mashed potatoes.

> 6   *Russet potatoes, scrubbed*
>
> 4   *tablespoons unsalted butter*
>
> 1   *pound parsnips, trimmed, peeled, and
>   cut into 2-inch chunks*
>
> 2   *tablespoons fresh thyme leaves*
>   *Freshly ground pepper*
>   *Salt*
>
> 2   *tablespoons pure maple syrup*
>
> 1   *bunch spinach, stemmed and washed*
>
> 1   *cup heavy cream*
>
> 3 to 4   *gratings whole nutmeg*
>
> 4   *egg whites, beaten into soft peaks*

1. Heat oven to 400°. Bake potatoes until fork tender, about 1 hour. Remove from oven, and let stand until cool enough to handle, about 20 minutes.

TWICE-BAKED POTATOES *are the perfect alternative to serving mashed or baked potatoes for a holiday meal. Here, parsnip soufflé puffs out of potato cups; the recipe also makes spinach soufflé. Serve guests one of each.*

2. Melt 2 tablespoons butter in a large roasting pan in preheated oven. Add the parsnips, thyme, 1/8 teaspoon pepper, and 1/2 teaspoon salt; stir to coat. Transfer pan to oven; cook until parsnips become soft, about 30 minutes.

3. Add maple syrup, and roast parsnips until they start to caramelize, about 10 minutes. Remove pan from oven; let cool slightly.

4. Transfer parsnips to a food mill. Run parsnips through mill, and set purée aside. Line a baking sheet with parchment; set aside.

5. Carefully slice potatoes in half crosswise, using a serrated knife to avoid tearing skin. Using a soupspoon, remove most of flesh from skins, leaving about 3/4 inch of flesh at bases. Set flesh of 2 whole potatoes aside for another use. Using serrated knife, trim bottoms of potatoes just enough so they sit flat, being careful to avoid making a hole through flesh. Transfer skins to sheet, cup-sides up.

6. Using a potato ricer or food mill, rice the remaining potato flesh into a clean mixing bowl. Cover bowl, and set aside.

7. Melt 1 tablespoon butter in a large skillet. Add spinach; season with 1 teaspoon salt and 1/4 teaspoon pepper. Cook over medium heat until spinach has wilted. Remove skillet from heat. Transfer spinach to bowl of food processor. Add 1/2 cup cream; process until smooth. Transfer mixture to mixing bowl.

8. Divide potato mixture in half. Add half to spinach mixture and half to parsnip purée.

9. Combine remaining 1/2 cup cream and 1 tablespoon butter in a small skillet. Cook over medium-low heat until butter has melted. Pour cream-butter mixture into parsnip purée. Season with 1/2 teaspoon salt and 1/8 teaspoon pepper. Add 3 to 4 gratings nutmeg to spinach mixture. Divide beaten egg whites in half; fold half into parsnip purée and half into spinach mixture until combined.

10. Using a spoon, fill six potato skins with spinach soufflé and six with parsnip soufflé, mounding so cups are just overflowing. Transfer baking sheet to oven; bake potatoes until hot, puffed, and golden brown, about 30 minutes. Serve immediately.

Lobster Newburg

SERVES 6

Newburg is a traditional New England dish of shellfish in a rich butter sauce flavored with sherry. You can cook the lobsters and make the stock (steps one through five) a day ahead.

> 3   *one-and-one-quarter-pound lobsters*
>
> 4   *tablespoons unsalted butter*
>
> 1   *medium onion, peeled and
>   coarsely chopped*
>
> 2   *stalks celery, coarsely chopped*
>
> 2   *medium leeks*
>
> 4   *medium carrots*
>
> 8   *fresh sprigs tarragon*
>
> 2   *tablespoons all-purpose flour*
>
> 1/4   *cup dry sherry*
>
> 2   *teaspoons tomato paste*
>
> 1/2   *cup heavy cream*
>
> 1   *teaspoon coarse salt*
>
> 1/8   *teaspoon freshly ground pepper*
>
> 1   *large egg yolk*

1. Fill a large stockpot three-quarters full with cold water. Set over high heat; bring to a rolling boil. Prepare an ice bath. Add lobsters to pot, making sure each lobster is completely submerged in water. Cook lobsters about 8 minutes. Using tongs, transfer lobsters to ice bath to cool. Drain lobsters in a colander.

2. Carefully remove lobster meat from the tails, claws, and legs, being careful to remove any cartilage from the claw meat. Cut the meat into bite-size pieces. Transfer meat to a bowl, cover with plastic, and refrigerate until ready to use. Discard lobster bodies, but reserve the shells from the tails, claws, and legs for making stock.

3. Melt 2 tablespoons butter in a large saucepan set over medium heat. Add chopped onion and celery to pan. Coarsely chop 1 leek and 2 carrots; add to pan. Add reserved lobster shells, 4 sprigs tarragon, and enough water to cover shells by 3 inches.

4. Bring liquid to a boil, reduce heat, and simmer, skimming surface often, until the stock is flavorful, about 1½ hours.

5. Prepare an ice bath. Strain stock through a fine sieve, pushing down on solids to extract liquid. Transfer stock to a clean saucepan, and discard solids. Continue cooking stock until liquid has reduced to 2 cups. Remove from heat, and transfer to ice bath to chill. Transfer chilled stock to an airtight container; refrigerate until ready to use.

6. Split the remaining leek lengthwise. Cut the leek and remaining 2 carrots into ½-inch pieces; set aside.

7. Melt the remaining 2 tablespoons butter in a medium saucepan set over medium-low heat. Sprinkle flour into saucepan; cook, stirring constantly, so mixture foams and forms a paste but does not turn brown, about 2 minutes.

8. Carefully add sherry, stirring constantly to loosen any flour that has cooked onto bottom of saucepan, being careful that no lumps form. Add tomato paste and 2 cups reserved lobster stock. Add chopped leek and carrot to saucepan, and cook until just tender, about 4 minutes. Stir in the cream, and bring to a boil. Reduce heat, and simmer until the sauce just starts to thicken, 5 to 6 minutes. Add the salt and pepper. Pick the tarragon from remaining 4 sprigs, chop, and add.

9. In a small bowl, whisk egg yolk. Add a ladleful of hot sauce to yolk; whisk to combine. Return mixture to saucepan over low heat; whisk to combine. Remove from heat.

10. Heat oven to 350°. Fill a large roasting pan with 1 inch boiling water; set six 6-ounce ramekins into pan.

11. Add reserved lobster meat to the sauce; stir to combine. Divide the Newburg evenly among ramekins. Transfer the roasting pan to oven, and cook until the Newburg bubbles, about 25 minutes. Remove roasting pan from the oven, and carefully transfer ramekins to serving plates. Serve immediately.

Wild-Rice Dressing

SERVES 12 TO 18

- ¼ cup slivered almonds
  Unsalted butter, for casserole
- 3 tablespoons plus 1 teaspoon olive oil
- 1 medium onion, coarsely chopped
- 2 celery stalks, chopped into ½-inch pieces
- 3 large cloves garlic, minced
- 1 tablespoon finely chopped fresh rosemary
- 1 tablespoon finely chopped fresh sage
  Salt and freshly ground pepper
- 2 tablespoons coarsely chopped flat-leaf parsley
- 4 ounces sweet fennel sausage, casings removed
- 1 Granny Smith apple, peeled, cored, and cut into ½-inch dice
- ¼ cup Calvados or white wine
- 3 cups cooked wild rice
- 2 cups cooked white rice
- 10 dried apricot halves, quartered
- 6 dried pitted prunes, halved

1. Heat oven to 375°. Spread almonds on a baking pan; toast until golden, 5 to 7 minutes. Remove from oven; set almonds aside to cool.

2. Butter a 2½-quart casserole; set aside. Heat 2 tablespoons olive oil in a large sauté pan over medium heat. Add onion, celery, and garlic. Cook, until tender, about 7 minutes.

3. Increase heat to high; add rosemary, sage, salt, and pepper. Continue cooking until vegetables are golden, 2 to 3 minutes. Remove pan from heat; stir in the parsley. Transfer to a large bowl; set aside. Return pan to heat.

4. Crumble sausage. Add 1½ teaspoons olive oil to pan. Cook sausage, stirring and breaking up meat until well browned, 2½ to 3 minutes. Transfer to bowl with reserved vegetables. Return pan to heat.

5. Add remaining 1½ teaspoons olive oil to pan. Add apple; cook until browned, 2 to 3 minutes. Add Calvados. Using a wooden spoon, scrape up any brown bits on bottom of pan. Cook until most of liquid has evaporated, about 1 minute.

6. Remove pan from heat, and transfer mixture to bowl with sausage and vegetables. Add wild and white rice, apricots, prunes, and reserved toasted almonds. Season with salt and pepper. Transfer dressing to prepared casserole; cover with aluminum foil. The dressing may be made one day in advance and refrigerated. If made ahead, warm in a 275° oven until hot, 30 to 40 minutes, before spooning into the crown roast.

Warm String-Bean Salad

SERVES 6

Martha likes to chop the beans to make them look like tiny jewels. They can also be cooked whole.

- 1½ pounds mixed beans, such as green beans, yellow beans, and haricots verts
  Salt
- 2 tablespoons unsalted butter
  Freshly ground pepper
- 1 cup loosely packed flat-leaf parsley, coarsely chopped
  Grated zest of 1 lemon

1. Trim the stems and tips of green beans, yellow beans, and haricots verts. Cut all beans into ¼-inch pieces.

2. Bring a large stockpot of water to a boil. Add 1¼ teaspoons salt and the beans. Cook the beans until tender, about 2 minutes. Transfer the beans to a colander to drain.

3. Melt the butter in a large skillet set over medium heat. Add the beans; season with salt and pepper. Cook, stirring often, until beans are hot and coated in butter, about 2 minutes. Add the parsley and the grated lemon zest; stir to combine. Serve.

Crown Roast

A good butcher can prepare a crown roast for you in advance, but adventurous cooks may want to try it at home.
Technically, a crown roast comes from the rib-chop section of a rack of pork. If you want to make it at home, have
the butcher remove the chine and feather bones and any excess fat from the rack, and you can take it from there.

CROWN ROAST *makes an impressive presentation.*
You can add to the spectacle by serving dressing in
the center of the crown. To serve the roast, carefully lift
it out of the pan, place on a serving platter, and carve.

Crown Roast With Gravy

SERVES 12 TO 18

For the most succulent roast, the meat and dressing
must be cooked separately. If the roast is stuffed
before cooking, the meat will be tough and dry,
because the dressing requires longer to cook.

- 1 eight-to-nine-pound crown roast of pork
  Salt and freshly ground pepper
- 5½ tablespoons olive oil
  Grated zest of 1 orange
- 4 large cloves garlic, minced
- 2 tablespoons chopped fresh rosemary
  Wild-Rice Dressing (recipe, page 115)
- ¾ cup dry white wine
- ½ cup fresh apple cider
- 1½ cups veal or chicken stock,
  preferably homemade
- 1 tablespoon unsalted butter,
  room temperature
- 2 tablespoons all-purpose flour

1. Heat oven to 425°. Position rack in lower third of oven. Season meat with salt and pepper; brush meat with 4 tablespoons olive oil.
2. In a small bowl, combine the orange zest, garlic, rosemary, and the remaining 1½ tablespoons olive oil. Spread the mixture evenly over the meat, inside and out.
3. Place meat in a heavy-duty roasting pan with a rack large enough to hold roast without crowding sides. Roast 15 minutes. Reduce heat to 375°. Continue roasting, rotating pan after 45 minutes, until meat is well browned and an instant-read thermometer registers 150°, about 1½ hours. (Insert thermometer into meaty center of the crown, making sure it does not touch any ribs. Take several readings to ensure temperature is even all around.)
4. While crown roast is cooking, make Wild-Rice Dressing. Remove roast from oven, transfer to a cutting board with a well, and let stand 20 minutes. Raise oven temperature to 425°. Place dressing in oven; bake until heated through, about 20 minutes. Pour pan juices into a fat separator or glass measuring cup; let stand 5 to 10 minutes. If using a separator, carefully pour juice back into pan; discard fat. If using a measuring cup, carefully remove fat with a spoon, and return juices to pan.
5. Place roasting pan on top of stove over medium-high heat. Add the wine; bring to a boil. Using a wooden spoon, stir up any brown bits on bottom of pan. Boil until half of liquid has evaporated, 5 to 7 minutes. Stir in apple cider and veal stock; season with salt and pepper, and return liquid to a boil.
6. In a small bowl, combine butter with flour. Mix until completely combined. Transfer to roasting pan. Whisk constantly until gravy has slightly thickened, 4 to 5 minutes. Remove pan from heat; strain liquid into a gravy boat.
7. Carefully transfer roast from cutting board to a serving platter; spoon dressing into center of the roast, and carve.

1. Along with the rack of pork cut in two sections, assemble your tools: You'll need a boning knife to trim the rib bones—or french the chops, as it's called; a larger knife; and a sharpening steel. You'll need cotton kitchen twine to thread racks together and a barding needle for the threading.

2. With the larger knife, make an indentation perpendicular to the bone of the first rack, about 1½ to 2 inches from end of bone.

3. Continue with second rack by lining it up with the indentation in first rack so that they will be even.

4. Cut away excess meat between incisions and ends of bones. Make sure the cut is deep enough to expose the bones. Reserve this excess meat for another use.

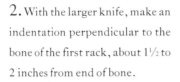
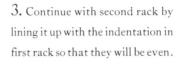

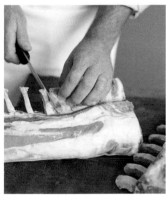

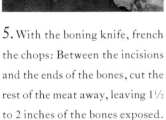

5. With the boning knife, french the chops: Between the incisions and the ends of the bones, cut the rest of the meat away, leaving 1½ to 2 inches of the bones exposed.

6. Lay rack down with the meaty side of the chops faceup. Make an incision between every two chops, about a third of the way through. This will give you the flexibility to bend the chops into a circle.

7. Stand the racks up, chop-sides down, and bend them into a circle. Using needle and twine, join the two end chops together with two separate ties, one about 1 inch below the exposed bones and the second 2 to 3 inches below that. Tighten the twine until the chops are evenly spaced, and tie off with a simple knot. Repeat at the opposite side of the crown. You are now ready to roast.

8. Prepare the crown roast of pork as you would any other roast; begin by seasoning with salt and pepper, and brush meat with 4 tablespoons olive oil. In small bowl, combine orange zest, garlic, rosemary, and remaining 1½ tablespoons olive oil. Spread mixture evenly over the meat, inside and out. Roast as directed in recipe.

Lardy Cake

MAKES TWO 11-BY-17-INCH CAKES

Martha was inspired to develop this recipe after sampling a huge lardy cake at the Flour Bag Bakery in Gloucestershire, England. In the North of England, it is traditional to serve lardy cake on holidays and special occasions.

    Sour Lardy-Cake Dough (recipe follows)
    All-purpose flour, for rolling out dough
- 2 tablespoons ground ginger
- 2 tablespoons ground cinnamon
- 2 teaspoons ground coriander
- 1/2 teaspoon ground nutmeg
- 1/2 teaspoon ground mace
- 6 cups mixed dried fruit, such as currants, cranberries, and golden raisins
- 8 ounces pure vegetable shortening
- 1 1/2 cups turbinado or packed light-brown sugar
- 1/2 cup apricot jam
- 1/4 cup cognac

1. Using a rolling pin, roll out half of the dough on a lightly floured work surface into a 16-inch square. Cover remaining half with plastic; set aside. In a small bowl, combine spices. In a large bowl, combine dried fruit.
2. Spread 2 ounces shortening over top of dough, leaving a 1/2-inch border around perimeter. Sprinkle 6 tablespoons brown sugar over shortening. Sprinkle one-fourth of combined spices over sugar. Sprinkle one-fourth of dried fruit over spices. Using palms of your hands, gently press fruit into dough.
3. Fold four corners of square into center, creating a smaller square, enclosing filling. Gently press down on dough with rolling pin. Spread 2 ounces shortening over dough, leaving a 1/2-inch border around perimeter. Sprinkle 6 tablespoons sugar, another one-fourth of spices, and another one-fourth of fruit. Using palms of your hands, gently press fruit into dough; fold dough into thirds.
4. Transfer dough to a piece of parchment paper; roll out into an 11-by-17-inch rectangle. Carefully lifting parchment, transfer to baking sheet. Let stand about 20 minutes.
5. Repeat steps one through four with remaining dough, shortening, brown sugar, spices, and dried fruit.

6. Heat oven to 350°. Combine jam and cognac in a small saucepan. Set over low heat; cook until liquefied. Strain jam; discard solids. Brush surface of lardy cakes with jam.
7. Bake cakes until golden and puffed, 35 to 45 minutes. Let cool slightly before serving. Lardy cake will keep up to 1 day, wrapped in foil; reheat cake before serving.

Sour Lardy-Cake Dough

MAKES ENOUGH FOR 2 CAKES

Once this dough is prepared, make the Lardy cake.

- 5 teaspoons active dry yeast
- 3 cups sponge (recipe follows), pulled into small pieces
- 4 cups bread flour
- 1 tablespoon salt
- All-purpose flour, for rolling out dough
- Vegetable oil, for bowl

1. In the bowl of an electric mixer fitted with the paddle attachment, combine 1 cup warm water (110°) and yeast. Let stand until creamy, about 10 minutes. Add 1/2 cup warm water and the sponge. Mix on low speed until combined, about 2 minutes.
2. In a medium bowl, combine flour and salt. Add to yeast mixture, and mix on low speed 1 minute. Change attachment to dough hook, and mix on medium-low speed until dough is smooth and just sticks to your fingers when squeezed, about 8 minutes.
3. Lightly flour a work surface. Turn out dough, and knead 4 or 5 turns into a ball. Place dough, smooth side up, in a lightly oiled bowl, and cover with plastic wrap. Let rise in a warm place until dough has doubled and is slightly blistered and satiny, about 1 hour.
4. Punch dough down, and fold over 4 or 5 times. Place folded side facedown in bowl. Cover, and let rise again in a warm place until doubled in bulk and satiny, about 50 minutes. Divide dough in half, and wrap in plastic until ready to use.

Sponge

MAKES ABOUT 3 1/2 CUPS

Sponge is a mixture of yeast, flour, and water that, when allowed to sit, bubbles and ferments; used in bread, it imparts a tangy flavor.

- 1/2 teaspoon active dry yeast
- 3 1/2 cups all-purpose flour
- Vegetable oil, for bowl

1. In the bowl of an electric mixer, combine 1/4 cup warm water (110°) and yeast. Let stand until creamy, about 10 minutes.
2. Add 1 1/4 cups warm water and flour; mix on low speed, 2 minutes; the sponge should feel like a very wet dough.
3. Place sponge in a lightly oiled bowl. Cover with plastic wrap; let stand at room temperature 24 hours. Store sponge, refrigerated, up to 1 week, or freeze in plastic up to 3 months. Bring sponge to room temperature before using.

Torie's Chocolate-Chunk Toffee Cookies

MAKES ABOUT 2 1/2 DOZEN

Torie Hallock makes these delicious cookies at Martha's house in Maine. Toffee pieces can be found in the baking sections of grocery stores; if not, use the small pieces of Skor or Heath bars sold in bags.

- 1 1/2 cups all-purpose flour
- 1 teaspoon baking soda
- 1 cup (2 sticks) unsalted butter, room temperature
- 3/4 cup packed light-brown sugar
- 3/4 cup granulated sugar
- 1 large egg
- 1 teaspoon pure vanilla extract
- 1 1/2 cups oats
- 1 cup dried cherries
- 4 1/2 ounces bittersweet chocolate, coarsely chopped
- 1 cup (about 7 ounces) toffee pieces, finely chopped

1. Heat oven to 350°. Line two baking sheets with parchment; set aside. In a large bowl, sift together flour and baking soda.

2. In the bowl of an electric mixer fitted with the paddle attachment, cream the butter and both sugars on medium-high speed until light and fluffy, 2 to 3 minutes, scraping down the sides of the bowl once or twice during mixing. Add the egg; mix on high speed to combine. Add the vanilla; mix to combine. Scrape down the sides of the bowl.

3. Working in additions, add the flour mixture to the egg mixture on low speed until well combined. Add the oats, cherries, chocolate, and toffee pieces; mix to combine.

4. Spoon a heaping tablespoon of dough onto baking sheet. Repeat, spacing 2 inches apart.

5. Bake cookies until golden brown, about 10 minutes. Transfer to a wire rack to cool. Store in an airtight container up to 2 days.

Chocolate-Applesauce Cake

SERVES 8 TO 10

This moist cake is even better the day after it is made.

- 1 cup (2 sticks) unsalted butter, plus more for pan
- 2 cups granulated sugar
- 2 large eggs
- 2½ cups unsweetened applesauce, preferably homemade
- 1¾ cups all-purpose flour
- 1 cup unsweetened cocoa powder
- 1 teaspoon ground cinnamon
- ½ teaspoon ground nutmeg
- 1 teaspoon ground ginger
  Pinch of salt
- 2 teaspoons baking powder
- 1 teaspoon pure vanilla extract
- 2 tablespoons Calvados or brandy
- 6 ounces bittersweet chocolate, chopped into ½-inch pieces
- 1 tablespoon confectioners' sugar
  Cider Glaze, Apple Chips, and Crystallized Ginger (recipe follows)
- 2 cups whipped cream (optional)

1. Heat oven to 325°. Brush a 9½-inch kugelhopf ring mold (see the Guide) or Bundt pan with soft butter. Set mold aside.

2. In the bowl of an electric mixer fitted with the paddle attachment, combine the butter and granulated sugar. Beat on medium speed, scraping down the sides with a rubber spatula, until mixture is light and fluffy, about 5 minutes. Add the eggs, and beat 2 to 3 minutes more. Fold in the applesauce, being careful not to overmix.

3. In a large bowl, sift together the flour, cocoa powder, cinnamon, nutmeg, ginger, salt, and baking powder.

4. Fold the flour mixture into the applesauce mixture. Add the vanilla, Calvados, and chocolate pieces; mix until just combined. Pour batter into prepared pan; use a rubber spatula to clean bowl and smooth top.

5. Bake until cake pulls away from sides of pan and is springy to the touch or until a cake tester inserted into center comes out clean, about 2 hours. Transfer to a wire rack to cool slightly; turn out cake; let cool completely.

6. Sift confectioners' sugar over cooled cake. Pour cider glaze over top of cake, allowing to drip down sides. Garnish with apple chips and crystallized ginger. Serve cake with whipped cream, if desired.

Cider Glaze, Apple Chips, and Crystallized Ginger

GARNISHES 1 CAKE

- 2 cups apple cider
- 4 cups confectioners' sugar, sifted
- 2 lemons
- 2 Cortland or other firm red apples
- 1 two-inch piece fresh ginger, peeled

1. Combine cider and 1 cup confectioners' sugar in a small saucepan. Set over medium heat, and bring to a boil. Skim surface, removing any cider sediment that rises to the top. Reduce heat; simmer until liquid begins to thicken into a glaze, about 30 minutes.

2. Heat oven to 200°. Squeeze juice from lemons into a small bowl filled with cold water. Using a very sharp knife, slice apples into rounds as thinly as possible. Place rounds in acidulated water. Line baking sheet with a Silpat baking mat (see the Guide); set sheet aside.

3. Remove cider glaze from heat, and let stand until cool enough to touch. Carefully dip each apple round into the glaze, and place on the baking sheet.

4. Bake the apple rounds until they turn golden and the edges have curled, about 2 hours. Transfer apples to a wire rack, and let cool until crisp. Brush with the cider glaze.

5. Return cider glaze to heat. Slice ginger into ⅛ inch thick slices crosswise, and add to cider. Cook over low heat until ginger is soft and translucent, about 30 minutes. Using a slotted spoon, transfer ginger to wire rack to cool. The liquid should have reduced to be just less than ¾ cup.

6. Return glaze to heat; whisk in remaining 3 cups confectioners' sugar. Remove from heat. To test, pour a small amount over top of cake. If glaze is too thin, let cool slightly. If it is too thick, add a little more cider. Use when desired consistency is achieved.

MENU

cocktails
champagne

pear-pecan toasts

dinner
garlic thyme popovers

crispy Waldorf salad

brussels sprouts
with red onions

roast goose

dessert
holiday fig roll

dried-fruit compote

Christmas cupcakes

PARTY PLAN

TWO DAYS BEFORE
Make dried-fruit compote.
Make candied kumquats.

ONE DAY BEFORE
Transfer frozen goose to refrigerator to thaw.
Make popover batter.
Make wild-rice dressing.
Make holiday fig roll.

MORNING OF PARTY
Make cheese spread for toasts.
Combine sliced vegetables for salad.

TWO HOURS BEFORE
Put goose in oven.

JUST BEFORE
Make pear-pecan toasts.
Toss salad.
Make brussels sprouts with red onions.
Warm dressing.

LAST THING
Bake popovers.

Pear-Pecan Toasts

SERVES 6 TO 8

Look for small pears, or trim the pear slices to fit on the toast.

- 6 ounces Roquefort cheese
- 3 tablespoons heavy cream
- 8 slices white sandwich bread, crusts removed
- 1 Bartlett or other firm pear, thinly sliced into wedges
- 16 pecan halves, toasted

1. Heat oven to 350°. In a small bowl, combine the cheese and heavy cream. Using a fork or wooden spoon, combine until mixture is soft enough to spread but not too runny; set aside.

2. Cut bread in half crosswise, making finger sandwiches that are about 3 by 1½ inches. Transfer bread fingers to a baking sheet; toast in oven until light golden on each side, about 6 minutes per side. Remove.

3. Spread 1 heaping teaspoon cheese mixture on each bread finger. Top with a pear slice; garnish with pecan half. Serve at room temperature.

Garlic Thyme Popovers

MAKES 1 DOZEN

Popover batter may be made up to one day ahead and refrigerated. Popover tins (see the Guide) are special pans that allow the hot air to circulate fully around each popover, creating a more dramatic pop; regular muffin tins may be used with smaller results.

- 2½ tablespoons goose fat or pure vegetable shortening, plus more for pans
- 3 small cloves garlic, minced
- 2½ tablespoons chopped fresh thyme
- 2 tablespoons unsalted butter, melted
- 2 cups milk
- 2 cups all-purpose flour
- 2 teaspoons salt
- 5 large eggs

1. Heat oven to 450°. Place rack on bottom level. Lightly coat either two 6-cup popover tins, or a 12-cup muffin tin with 3-inch-diameter cups with the fat; set aside.

2. Heat 1½ teaspoons of the fat in a small sauté pan over low heat. Add garlic; cook until soft, about 3 minutes. Add thyme; set aside.

3. In an 8-cup glass measuring bowl, whisk together melted butter, milk, flour, and salt. Slightly beat eggs; gradually whisk into milk mixture. Whisk in reserved thyme and garlic. Batter may be made up to this point up to one day ahead.

4. Heat empty tins for 5 minutes; remove from oven. Divide remaining 2 tablespoons fat among tins, and heat until fat sizzles, about 10 minutes. Quickly pour batter evenly among cups, about halfway up the side of each.

5. Bake for 15 minutes; reduce heat to 350° without opening the oven. Continue baking until popovers puff up and are golden brown, about 15 minutes more. When done, sides should feel crisp and firm. Poke with a sharp knife to release steam; serve immediately.

Crispy Waldorf Salad

MAKES 6 TO 8 SERVINGS

- 1 cup pecans
- 1 one-pound fennel bulb, trimmed
- 2 tablespoons plus 1 teaspoon freshly squeezed lemon juice
- 1 Granny Smith apple
- 1 medium bunch seedless red grapes, halved (about 1½ cups)
- 4 stalks celery, strings removed, thinly sliced crosswise
- 6 to 8 escarole leaves, stacked, cut crosswise into thin strips
- ¼ cup chopped dill
- ¼ cup plain yogurt
- 2 tablespoons extra-virgin olive oil
  Salt and freshly ground pepper

1. Heat oven to 350°. Spread pecans on a baking pan. Bake until golden and fragrant, 10 to 15 minutes. Cool on a wire rack. Halve pecans; set aside.

2. Very thinly slice fennel bulb using a mandoline or a sharp knife. Transfer to a large bowl; add 1 teaspoon of lemon juice, and toss.

3. Cut apple, with skin on, into thin wedges; add to fennel, and toss with lemon juice. Add the grapes, celery, escarole, and half the dill to bowl. Toss to combine. Salad may be made up to this point up to 4 hours ahead.

4. In a small bowl, combine 2 tablespoons lemon juice, yogurt, olive oil, and salt and pepper to taste. Drizzle vinaigrette over the salad, using only as much as needed to lightly coat the salad. Transfer to a serving bowl; garnish with remaining dill and the pecans.

Brussels Sprouts With Red Onions

SERVES 6 TO 8

- 4 strips bacon
- 12 ounces red pearl onions, trimmed
- 2 pounds brussels sprouts, trimmed and halved
- 2/3 cup homemade chicken stock or 1 fourteen-ounce can low-sodium chicken stock
- 2 teaspoons chopped fresh oregano or rosemary
  Salt and freshly ground pepper

1. Cook bacon over medium heat in a large skillet until fat is rendered and bacon is cooked through. Transfer to paper towel to drain. Leave bacon fat in skillet.

2. Add pearl onions to skillet; cook over medium heat shaking pan from time to time to ensure even caramelization. Cook 5 minutes. Add brussels sprouts, flat-side down; cook until golden-brown on flat side, about 5 minutes. Turn over, and add chicken stock. Cook, covered, for 5 minutes on medium-low heat. Uncover and cook until liquid has reduced to a few tablespoons and vegetables are tender, about 8 minutes more.

3. Chop bacon into small pieces; add to pan. Add oregano. Season with salt and pepper. Serve hot.

Roast Goose

Goose is almost as simple to cook as chicken; it requires just a few ingredients to enhance its flavor, as well as some kitchen twine to tie the legs. A twelve-pound goose should provide enough meat to serve six people. If the goose is frozen, as are almost all geese these days, allow it to thaw overnight in the refrigerator.

TO CARVE THE GOOSE (top), *pull one leg away from body, and cut through joint. Remove other leg the same way. Find breast bone, and cut down along one side between breast bone and meat until you reach wing joint. Cut meat away from breast bone and rib cage. Arrange several slices on a plate (above), with dressing and brussels sprouts.*

Roast Goose

SERVES 6

1 twelve-pound fresh or frozen goose, giblets reserved
   Salt and freshly ground pepper to taste
3 medium carrots, halved
3 stalks celery, halved
1 head garlic, halved crosswise
1 bunch fresh thyme sprigs
1 bunch fresh sage
1 medium onion, halved
8 sprigs fresh flat-leaf parsley
1 dried bay leaf
1 teaspoon whole black peppercorns
½ cup dry white wine
1 tablespoon unsalted butter
   Wild-Rice Dressing (recipe, page 115)

1. If the goose is frozen, place it in the refrigerator overnight to thaw. Remove the goose from the refrigerator, and let it stand at room temperature for 30 minutes. Heat the oven to 400°. Rinse the goose inside and out with cold running water, and pat it dry with paper towels. Trim as much of the excess fat as possible from the opening of the cavity. Remove the first and second joints of the wings, and set them aside for use in making the stock.

2. With the point of a sharp knife, prick the entire surface of the goose skin, being careful not to cut into the flesh. Fold the neck flap under the body of the goose, and pin the flap down with a wooden toothpick. Generously sprinkle the cavity with salt and pepper, and insert two carrot halves, two celery-stalk halves, garlic, thyme, and sage. Using a piece of kitchen twine, tie the legs together. Generously sprinkle the outside of the goose with salt and pepper, and place it, breast-side up, on a wire rack set in a large roasting pan.

3. Roast the goose in the oven until it turns a golden brown, about 1 hour. With a baster, remove as much fat as possible from the roasting pan every 30 minutes. Reduce the heat to 325°, and roast until the goose is very well browned all over and an instant-read thermometer inserted into a breast, not touching a bone, registers 180°, about 1 hour after reducing the temperature.

4. Meanwhile, prepare goose stock, which will be used when making the gravy. Trim and discard any excess fat from the wing tips, neck, and giblets, and place them in a small stockpot. Add four carrot halves, four celery-stalk halves, both onion halves, parsley, bay leaf, peppercorns, and enough water to cover the bones and vegetables by 1 inch (about 2½ quarts water). Place the stockpot over high heat, and bring to a boil. Reduce heat to medium low, and simmer stock, skimming the scum as it forms, for 2 hours. Strain stock through a cheesecloth-lined strainer. Remove and discard the fat floating on the surface of the stock, and set the stockpot aside.

5. Remove the goose from the oven, and transfer it to a cutting board that has a well. Let the goose stand 15 to 20 minutes.

6. Meanwhile, prepare the gravy. Pour off all the fat from the roasting pan, and place the pan over high heat. Pour in the wine, and cook, stirring up any brown bits with a wooden spoon until the cooking liquid is reduced by three-quarters. Add 2 cups goose stock, and cook, stirring until the liquid is again reduced by three-quarters. Season with salt and pepper to taste. Stir in butter; cook until slightly thickened. Pass gravy through a cheesecloth-lined strainer into a gravy boat, and serve with the goose. Serve with the dressing.

PREPARATION

1. Geese are generously endowed with fat, so trim away as much of it as possible before cooking. You can remove between a third and a half pound from the cavity alone. Even so, plenty will remain, enough to keep the meat moist and to require draining every 30 minutes as the goose roasts.

2. Since the wings contain so little meat, the first and second joints should be removed before cooking; otherwise, they will burn. Save the wings to make goose stock, which will be used to make the gravy.

3. With the point of a sharp knife, prick the entire surface of the skin to release the fat as it melts during cooking. Be careful not to cut into the flesh, which would cause the meat to dry out.

4. Turn the goose breast-side down, and fold the flap of neck skin over the body, pinning it down with a toothpick so that the skin will not dangle. Turn the goose breast-side up again.

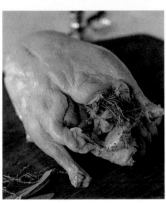  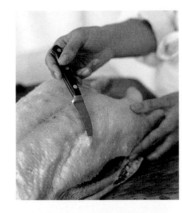 

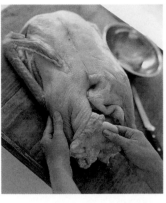   

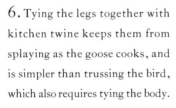 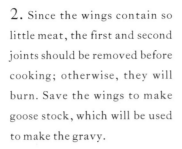

5. Salt and pepper the cavity of the goose, and then insert one carrot, one celery stalk, a head of garlic cut lengthwise, fresh thyme, and fresh sage. As it cooks, the goose will absorb the aromas and flavors. Do not stuff the goose with dressing. Because of the amount of fat that drips as the bird roasts, dressing is best cooked separately.

6. Tying the legs together with kitchen twine keeps them from splaying as the goose cooks, and is simpler than trussing the bird, which also requires tying the body.

7. As goose cooks, remove fat with a baster. To retain fat for future use, strain it through cheesecloth; set aside. Place fat in a covered jar; refrigerate. Make sure fat is free of liquid and clean of residue, and it will keep for months. The goose is done when well-browned and breast registers 180°. Transfer to a cutting board with a well; let stand 20 minutes before carving to allow juices to settle.

8. Meanwhile, make the simple but delicious gravy. Pour off any remaining fat from the pan, and place the pan over high heat. Add dry white wine, and stir up any brown bits that are stuck to the bottom with a wooden spoon. Add goose stock, and continue to stir until gravy thickens. Add salt and pepper, stir in the butter, and strain through cheesecloth.

Holiday Fig Roll

SERVES 16

To get a nice log shape, lay the cake on a kitchen towel, fill it, roll it, then clip the towel's ends together with clothespins until the cake sets. You may substitute cream cheese for the mascarpone; add two more tablespoons confectioners' sugar and half a teaspoon vanilla.

FOR THE CAKE:

- ½ cup unsalted butter (1 stick), melted and cooled, plus more for pan and foil
- 1 pound soft dried figs (see the Guide), stems removed, quartered
- ¼ cup dried currants (see the Guide)
- 1½ cups milk
- 1½ cups all-purpose flour
- ¾ cup firmly packed light-brown sugar
- 2½ teaspoons baking powder
- 1 teaspoon ground cinnamon
- ½ teaspoon freshly grated nutmeg
- ¼ teaspoon ground ginger
- ¼ teaspoon ground cloves
- ½ teaspoon salt
- 3 slices white bread
- 4 large eggs
- 2 tablespoons chopped Candied Kumquats (optional, recipe follows)
- 2 tablespoons crystallized ginger (optional, see the Guide)

FOR THE FILLING AND GARNISH:

- 2 pounds mascarpone cheese (see the Guide)
- ½ cup heavy cream
- ½ cup confectioners' sugar
  Dried Fruit Compote (recipe follows)
  Candied Kumquats for garnish (optional)

1. FOR THE CAKE: Heat oven to 350°. Butter an 18-by-12-inch jelly-roll pan. Line with parchment paper, and butter the parchment. Place figs, dried currants, and milk in medium saucepan; bring to a simmer over medium heat. Cook until liquid is absorbed, 8 to 10 minutes. Mixture will become grainy. Remove from heat, place mixture in bowl of food processor, and process until it is a thick paste (it should not be completely smooth). Set aside.

2. Sift flour, brown sugar, baking powder, cinnamon, nutmeg, ginger, cloves, and salt into a medium bowl; set aside. Tear bread into small pieces; place in the bowl of a food processor. Pulse until even crumbs form, about 10 pulses, to yield about 1½ cups bread crumbs.

3. Place eggs in the bowl of an electric mixer fitted with the paddle attachment; beat on high speed until frothy. Add reserved fig mixture, bread crumbs, kumquats, ginger, and melted butter. Mix until combined. With mixer on low speed, add reserved flour mixture; mix until just combined.

4. Bring about 3 cups water to a boil in a medium saucepan. Using an offset spatula, spread batter as evenly as possible in prepared pan. Cover pan loosely with buttered foil, and place on middle rack in oven. Place a baking pan filled with the boiling water on rack beneath cake. Bake until cake is springy and a cake tester comes out clean, about 40 minutes, rotating once halfway through baking time. Remove from oven, and set on a cooling rack for only 10 minutes. Lay a clean kitchen towel and a sheet pan over cake, and invert. Allow to cool for 10 minutes. Allow roll to remain wrapped in towel for 10 minutes. Unroll, and cool to room temperature. Don't worry if there are some breaks in the cake; once filled it can be rolled with cracked pieces on bottom.

5. FOR THE FILLING: Combine mascarpone, cream, and confectioners' sugar in a large bowl; fold until smooth. Place mixture in refrigerator until ready to use; it will be easier to roll cake if cheese mixture is cold. Using an offset spatula, spread chilled mascarpone mixture evenly over cake. Roll up again inside kitchen towel, forming a 17½-inch-long log. Leaving cake ends exposed, bring towel's edges up over top of cake, and roll, applying pressure to sides. Secure with clothespins or plastic binder clips to make a cylindrical log shape. Chill rolled cake for at least 4 hours, or overnight. Allow to stand at room temperature for 30 minutes before serving.

6. Just before serving, trim ends of the cake, forming a 16-inch-long log. Slice into 1-inch-thick servings. Garnish with dried-fruit compote and candied kumquats, if desired.

Dried-Fruit Compote

MAKES ENOUGH FOR 1 FIG ROLL

Make this compote up to three days ahead and keep, refrigerated, in an airtight container. Return to room temperature before using, or compote may be warmed slightly in a small saucepan over low heat. Look for light and dark dried figs to put in the compote.

- 2 cups sugar
- 8 ounces dried figs, halved
- 2 ounces dried currants
- 4 ounces golden raisins
- 2 ounces crystallized ginger (see the Guide), cut into ½-inch pieces if needed
- 4 ounces glacé pears (see the Guide) or dried pears, cut in half lengthwise
- 4 ounces Candied Kumquats (recipe follows)
- 1 cup cider
- 5 cinnamon sticks
- 7 whole cloves

1. Combine the sugar with 2 cups of water in a medium saucepan. Cover and bring to a boil over medium-high heat, stirring often until sugar dissolves. Transfer to a medium bowl and let cool to room temperature.

2. Combine the figs, currants, raisins, ginger, pears, kumquats, cider, cinnamon sticks, and cloves in a medium saucepan. Cover, and bring to a simmer over medium-low heat. Simmer 5 minutes. Stir in sugar syrup, and simmer until the fruits are translucent, about 1 hour. Let fruits cool in the syrup at room temperature. Serve over holiday fig roll.

Candied Kumquats

MAKES ABOUT 1½ CUPS

- 1 pint kumquats (see the Guide)
- 1½ cups sugar

1. Cut kumquats in half crosswise, and remove pits. Place in a medium saucepan with enough water to cover, and bring to a boil over medium-high heat. Drain in a fine strainer.

2. Place sugar and 1 cup water in a medium saucepan; bring to a boil. When all sugar has dissolved, reduce heat to very low, and add kumquats. Cover, and cook until kumquat skins are translucent, 1½ to 2 hours. Remove from heat; let cool to room temperature in the syrup. Candied kumquats can be stored in the syrup in an airtight container up to 3 days.

Christmas Cupcakes

MAKES 3 DOZEN

FOR THE CUPCAKES:

- 1½ cups cake flour (not self-rising), sifted
- ½ teaspoon baking powder
- ¼ teaspoon salt
- ¾ cup (1½ sticks) unsalted butter, room temperature
- 1 cup sugar
- 2 large eggs
- 1 teaspoon pure vanilla extract
- ½ teaspoon pure almond extract
- ½ cup nonfat buttermilk

FOR THE BUTTER GLAZE AND DECORATING:

- 2 cups sifted confectioners' sugar
- 8 tablespoons (1 stick) unsalted butter
- 8 teaspoons milk
- Royal Icing (recipe follows)

1. FOR THE CUPCAKES: Heat the oven to 350°. Line three twelve-holed mini-muffin tins with baking cups, and set aside. In a medium bowl, sift together flour, baking powder, and salt; set aside.

2. In the bowl of an electric mixer fitted with the paddle attachment, cream butter and sugar on medium speed until light and fluffy, about 3 minutes. Add eggs, one at a time, then the vanilla and almond extracts.

3. With mixer on low speed, add one-third of the reserved flour mixture, and mix until combined. Add ¼ cup buttermilk; combine.

Add another third of flour mixture, then the remaining ¼ cup buttermilk. Add the last third of flour, and mix until smooth.

4. Transfer batter to a pastry bag fitted with a coupler. Fill each baking cup three-quarters full. Using an offset spatula, carefully smooth the tops. Bake until a cake tester inserted into the middles comes out clean, about 18 minutes. Transfer muffin tins to a wire rack to cool. Remove cupcakes from tins.

5. FOR THE GLAZE: Place 1 cup confectioners' sugar in a medium bowl. In a small saucepan, melt 4 tablespoons butter over medium heat. Remove pan from heat; immediately pour butter into bowl with sugar. Add 4 teaspoons milk; whisk until smooth. Working quickly, dip the top of each cupcake into glaze, and place cupcake right side up on wire rack.

6. Repeat step five; glaze remaining cupcakes.

7. Allow glaze to set, about 20 minutes. Using a pastry bag fitted with a plain writing tip and filled with royal icing, decorate.

Royal Icing

MAKES 2½ CUPS

- 1 pound confectioners' sugar
- 3 large egg whites or 5 tablespoons meringue powder mixed with ½ cup water
- Paste or gel food coloring

In the bowl of an electric mixer fitted with the paddle attachment, combine confectioners' sugar and egg whites. Mix on medium-high speed until combined and thickened, about 8 minutes. If decorating with more than one color, divide icing into batches. Using the end of a toothpick, add food coloring until the desired shade is achieved.

Note: Raw eggs should not be used in food prepared for pregnant women, babies, young children, the elderly, or anyone whose health is compromised.

TINY CUPCAKES, *topped with butter glaze and royal icing, glisten with holiday decorations that are sure to catch the eyes of little guests.*

MENU

cocktails

pear-champagne **punch**

holiday **bloody Mary**

buffet

avocado grapefruit **salad**
with lime vinaigrette

smoked-**salmon** and
caramelized-onion stuffed celery stalks

sun-dried-tomato **palmiers**

twice-baked **cheese strudel**

lentil stars

choucroute garni

boeuf bourguignon with golden
mashed-potato crust

wild-mushroom and
spinach **lasagna**

dessert

Camembert stuffed
with pears and walnuts

pear tart

caramelized lemon tart

apricot lattice **cookies**

rugelach fingers

pecan-caramel **shortbread**

golden **popcorn** squares

congo bars

Shaker **lemon** bars

PARTY PLAN

ONE WEEK BEFORE
Make sun-dried-tomato palmiers.
Make twice-baked strudel.

THREE DAYS BEFORE
Make pear chips.

TWO DAYS BEFORE
Make cookies.

DAY BEFORE
Make pear tart and pâte sucrée.
Make lentils for lentil stars.
Make lasagna and boeuf bourguignon.

MORNING OF PARTY
Make caramelized lemon tart.
Toast stars for lentil stars.
Make choucroute.

THREE HOURS BEFORE
Mix bloody Mary.

TWO HOURS BEFORE
Section grapefruit.
Clean lettuce.

JUST BEFORE
Make champagne punch.
Put out salad ingredients for salad.
Prepare salmon and celery stalks.
Combine lentil stars.
*Top boeuf bourguignon with potatoes,
and bake.*
Prepare Camembert.

Pear-Champagne Punch

MAKES 8 SIX-OUNCE DRINKS

Pear nectar can be found in gourmet grocery stores.

- 3 *tablespoons pear nectar*
- 3 *tablespoons Poire William*
- 2 *750-ml bottles chilled champagne*
- 1 *recipe Pear Chips (recipe follows)*

Combine the pear nectar, Poire William, and cold champagne in a large pitcher. Gently stir, and serve cold in individual glasses, each garnished with a pear chip.

Pear Chips

MAKES ABOUT 1½ DOZEN

Use unblemished, slightly underripe fruit. These chips can be kept in an airtight container for several days.

- 1 *pear*
- ¾ *cup confectioners' sugar*

1. Heat oven to 200°. Place a Silpat (see the Guide) on a baking sheet. Using a Japanese mandoline (see the Guide) or very sharp knife, slice pears lengthwise into very thin translucent rounds. Do not worry about removing seeds or cores. Using a fine sieve, sprinkle the confectioners' sugar completely over both sides of each pear slice to coat well. Transfer slices to baking sheet. Bake until edges begin to ruffle, 1 to 1½ hours. Turn slices over; bake until golden brown, 1 to 1½ hours more.
2. Transfer chips to a wire rack in a single layer to cool and harden. Once completely cooled, chips may be stored in an airtight container between layers of parchment paper up to 3 days.

Holiday Bloody Mary

MAKES 8 EIGHT-OUNCE DRINKS

- 1 *forty-six-ounce can low-sodium tomato juice*
- 2 *tablespoon Tabasco*
- 1 *tablespoons freshly grated horseradish or 2 tablespoons prepared*
- ½ *cup freshly squeezed lemon juice*
- 16 *ounces (2 cups) vodka Ice*

In a large pitcher, combine the tomato juice, Tabasco, horseradish, lemon juice, and vodka. Stir well and serve right away with ice, or refrigerate, without ice, until very cold. May be made up to 3 hours ahead.

Avocado Grapefruit Salad With Lime Vinaigrette

SERVES 10 TO 12

Deconstructing the salad and serving it in separate bowls, instead of tossing it together, allows guests to compose their own salad and keeps all the ingredients crisp and fresh.

- 4 *ripe avocados*
- ½ *cup freshly squeezed lime juice (about 3 limes)*
- 4 *ruby-red grapefruit, peel and pith removed*
- 1 *tablespoon honey*
- ½ *cup extra-virgin olive oil*
- ½ *teaspoon crushed red-pepper flakes Salt and freshly ground pepper*
- 3 *heads lettuce (about 2 pounds)*
- 2 *pomegranates, seeds removed and reserved*

1. Cut avocados in half lengthwise, working around pit; twist to open. Remove pits; peel. Cut avocados into 1-inch pieces; toss in bowl with ¼ cup lime juice.
2. Slice grapefruit crosswise into ¼-inch-thick rounds; place in a second bowl.
3. Make vinaigrette; combine remaining ¼ cup lime juice and the honey in small bowl. Whisk in olive oil and red-pepper flakes; season with salt and pepper. Transfer to a glass cruet or small glass pitcher for the table.
4. Arrange lettuce in a large serving bowl. Season with salt and pepper.

5. Place pomegranate seeds in a serving bowl. Arrange all the ingredients, in their bowls, on the table with serving spoons, and serve.

Smoked-Salmon and Caramelized-Onion Stuffed Celery Stalks

SERVES 10-12

If you want to make only one kind of stuffed celery, double the salmon or the onion mixture and eliminate the other from the ingredients list.

- 1 *tablespoon olive oil*
- 1 *medium red onion, peeled, thinly sliced*
- 1 *teaspoon sugar*
- 8 *ounces whipped cream cheese*
- 5 *tablespoons white horseradish, squeezed of liquid*
- 5 *ounces smoked salmon*
- 1 *tablespoons finely snipped fresh dill, plus small tips for garnish*
- 9 *twelve-inch celery stalks, cut into 2-inch lengths with strings removed*

1. In a medium sauté pan, heat olive oil over medium heat. Add onions, and reduce heat to low. Cook, stirring occasionally, about 15 minutes. Add sugar, and continue cooking, stirring occasionally, until onions are golden and caramelized, about 30 minutes. Remove from heat, and set aside.
2. In a medium bowl, combine the cream cheese and horseradish, and divide mixture between two bowls; set one bowl aside. Coarsely chop a quarter of the salmon, add to the cheese mixture in one bowl, and mix to combine. Cut remaining salmon into thin slivers, and set aside. Mound the cavities of half the celery with the salmon filling. Garnish each stalk with a sliver of salmon and a sprig of dill.
3. Fill remaining celery stalks with the remaining reserved cheese mixture, garnish with caramelized onions, and serve.

Sun-Dried-Tomato Palmiers

SERVES 10 TO 12

Sun-dried-tomato halves can also be used in this recipe. Cover 15 halves with boiling water. Let stand until softened. Drain and purée in a food processor with 3 tablespoons olive oil. Alternatively, sun-dried tomatoes packed in olive oil can be used. Remove 15 halves from the oil, and process until puréed.

- 2 sheets frozen puff pastry, thawed
- 6 tablespoons ricotta cheese
- 6 tablespoons sun-dried-tomato paste
- 1 cup grated Parmesan cheese (4 ounces)

1. Heat oven to 425°. Roll out one sheet of pastry into a rectangle about 1/8-inch thick. Trim pastry to approximately 8 by 11 inches. Spread half the ricotta on pastry. Spread half the sun-dried-tomato paste on top. Sprinkle with half the Parmesan. Roll each long end of the pastry to the center of the rectangle, making sure the pastry is tight and even. Repeat process with the remaining sheet of pastry, ricotta, tomatoes, and Parmesan. Wrap rolls separately with plastic wrap, and transfer to the refrigerator until firm, about 30 minutes. Alternately, place rolls in the freezer for up to one month. When ready to bake, remove from freezer, and let stand at room temperature until slightly tempered, or until a sharp knife can slice through roll without compressing it, about 10 minutes.

2. Remove rolls from refrigerator, and slice crosswise into 3/8-inch-thick slices. Place palmiers 2 inches apart on a parchment-lined baking sheet. Bake until puffed and lightly golden, 8 to 9 minutes. Turn over, and bake until golden, 5 to 6 minutes. Let cool completely on wire rack.

Twice-Baked Cheese Strudel

SERVES 10 TO 12

Phyllo dough is very thin, quickly dries out, and becomes brittle. To prevent drying, keep the unused portion covered with damp paper towels.

- 7 sheets phyllo dough
- 8 tablespoons (1 stick) unsalted butter, melted
- 10 tablespoons finely grated Asiago cheese
- 12 tablespoons finely grated Parmesan cheese
- 10 tablespoons finely grated Pecorino Romano cheese
- 6 tablespoons poppy seeds, plus more for topping

1. Heat oven to 350°. Place one sheet phyllo on a clean surface, and brush evenly with butter. Repeat 2 more times. Sprinkle third layer of buttered phyllo evenly with 2 tablespoons of each cheese, and 2 tablespoons poppy seeds. Repeat process four more times until there are two layers with butter and five layers with cheeses and seeds.

2. Carefully roll up the pastry and filling lengthwise compactly. The roll should measure 1 1/2 to 2 inches in diameter. Brush the outside of the roll with butter, and sprinkle with remaining 2 tablespoons Parmesan and 1 tablespoon poppy seeds. Cut the roll in half, and transfer to a parchment-lined baking pan. Alternatively, wrap each half in plastic wrap, and place in freezer for up to one month. When ready to bake, remove plastic and bake on parchment-lined baking pan. Frozen strudel will take longer to brown, up to 35 minutes.

3. Bake until deep golden, 20 to 25 minutes. Remove from oven, and transfer to a wire rack until cool enough to handle.

4. Using a serrated knife, carefully slice the roll into 1/2-inch-thick slices, and return to baking pan cut-side down. Bake until golden throughout, about 10 minutes. Remove from oven, and serve warm or at room temperature.

Lentil Stars

MAKES 2 DOZEN

- 2 dozen slices white bread
- 2 tablespoons unsalted butter, melted
- 1/3 cup French lentils
- 1 cup chicken stock, preferably homemade
- 5 cloves garlic
- 10 sprigs fresh thyme
- 2 tablespoons vegetable oil
- 1 slice slab bacon, about 1 ounce
  Freshly ground pepper

1. Heat oven to 350°. Using a 2 1/2-inch star-shaped cookie cutter, cut a star from each slice of bread. Brush each star with melted butter, and place on a parchment-lined baking sheet. Toast until golden brown, 8 to 10 minutes. Transfer stars to a wire rack.

2. In a medium saucepan, place the lentils, chicken stock, 2 cloves garlic, and 7 thyme sprigs. Cover pan, and bring to a boil. Uncover, reduce heat to medium low, and simmer until lentils are tender, about 25 minutes. Pick leaves from remaining 3 thyme sprigs, and set leaves aside.

3. Meanwhile, thinly slice remaining 3 garlic cloves. Heat oil in a small skillet over medium heat. Add garlic; cook until lightly golden, about 2 minutes. Transfer to a paper towel.

4. Discard oil; return skillet to heat. Add bacon, and cook until crisp, 4 to 6 minutes. Drain on paper towel. Let cool, and dice finely. Add cooked lentils and diced bacon to hot skillet; toss well. Season with pepper.

5. Place 1 1/2 teaspoons lentil mixture on each toasted star. Garnish with a slice of garlic and a few reserved thyme leaves. Serve warm.

Choucroute Garni

SERVES 10 TO 12

5 to 6 pounds drained sauerkraut
25 whole black peppercorns (see the Guide)
1½ teaspoons coriander seeds
5 whole cloves
15 juniper berries (see the Guide)
6 sprigs fresh flat-leaf parsley
4 sprigs fresh thyme
2 bay leaves
½ cup goose fat (see the Guide)
4 medium onions, sliced ⅛-inch thick
1½ cups Riesling or other dry white wine
2 cups chicken stock, skimmed of fat
1 slab (1½ pounds) dry-salted bacon, rinsed and dried
1 slab (1½ pounds) smoked bacon
2 dry-salted pig's knuckles, about 1½ pounds
1 pound smoked pork butt
3 carrots, peeled
¼ cup finely minced garlic
2 teaspoons salt
8 small red potatoes, peeled
4 white veal sausages (weisswurst or bock wurst; about 4 ounces each)
4 smoked country sausages (bauerwurst; about 4 ounces each)
4 knackwurst sausages (about 4 ounces each)

1. Place sauerkraut in a colander set in the sink; rinse with warm water, and drain.
2. Make bouquet garni: Place peppercorns, coriander seeds, cloves, juniper berries, parsley, thyme, and bay leaves on square of cheesecloth; tie with kitchen twine.
3. Melt goose fat in very large Dutch oven (see the Guide) over medium heat. Add sliced onions; cook, stirring frequently, until onions are translucent but not brown, about 10 minutes.
4. Add wine, chicken stock, and 2 cups water to Dutch oven; stir to combine. Add dry-salted bacon, smoked bacon, pig's knuckles, pork butt, carrots, garlic, salt, and bouquet garni. Lay washed and drained sauerkraut on top of mixture in Dutch oven. Add enough cold water to bring liquid to 1 inch below sauerkraut. Cover, increase heat to high, and bring liquid to boil. Reduce heat to low; cook at strong simmer for 1½ hours.

5. Add potatoes; simmer, covered, until potatoes are just becoming tender, about 30 minutes more. Add sausages; simmer, covered, until heated through, about 10 minutes more.
6. Remove bouquet garni, and discard. To serve choucroute garni on platter, remove meat, potatoes, and carrots from Dutch oven. Drain sauerkraut, and place in middle of serving platter. Slice bacon and pork butt. Arrange meat, potatoes, and carrots around sauerkraut.

Boeuf Bourguignon With Golden Mashed-Potato Crust

SERVES 10 TO 12

5 pounds stewing beef, cut into 1-inch cubes
½ cup all-purpose flour
4 teaspoons salt, plus more for water
1½ teaspoons freshly ground pepper
8 tablespoons canola oil
1 bottle (750 ml) red Burgundy wine
8 ounces pancetta or thick bacon, cut into ¼-inch cubes
2 onions, cut into ⅛-inch-thick rounds
5 carrots (about 1 pound), peeled, cut into ¼-inch-thick rounds
3 parsnips (about 1 pound), peeled, cut into ¼-inch-thick rounds
1 bay leaf
3 sprigs fresh thyme
5 sprigs fresh flat-leaf parsley
10 whole black peppercorns (see the Guide)
4 pounds (8 to 10) Yukon gold potatoes, peeled, cut into ¼-inch-thick rounds
1½ cups heavy cream
¾ cup (1½ sticks) unsalted butter
½ teaspoon freshly grated nutmeg
1 pound pearl onions, peeled
1½ pounds button mushrooms, cleaned and cut in quarters
10 to 12 small sprigs fresh oregano for garnish

1. Place beef in large bowl. In small bowl, whisk together flour, 2 teaspoons salt, and 1 teaspoon pepper. Sprinkle flour mixture over beef; toss to coat beef evenly.
2. Heat 12-inch heavy-bottomed skillet over medium heat. Add about 1 tablespoon canola

oil; swirl to coat bottom of skillet. Heat oil to just below smoking point; test by placing one piece of beef in pan. It should sizzle the moment it touches pan. If beef spits, sputters, and smokes, pan is too hot; remove it from heat to cool. If beef does not sizzle, pan is not hot enough; wait a minute or two more. Brown beef in manageable batches, about eight: Arrange an eighth of the meat in skillet so cubes do not touch. Cook until dark crust has formed and beef easily releases from pan when lifted with tongs, about 3 minutes. Brown all sides of each piece this way. Transfer first batch of browned beef to large Dutch oven (see the Guide). Return skillet to heat. Deglaze skillet: Pour in an eighth of wine (about 3 ounces); use wooden spoon to loosen bits that have cooked on to skillet. Pour wine and deglazed juices into Dutch oven. Return skillet to heat. Quickly wipe out with paper towel. Add another tablespoon of canola oil; repeat process of browning beef cubes and deglazing skillet.
3. When last batch of beef is browned and skillet is deglazed, return skillet to medium-low heat. Add pancetta; cook, stirring occasionally, until golden brown, about 10 minutes. With slotted spoon, transfer pancetta to Dutch oven. Pour half the oil from skillet into small bowl; set aside. In oil that remains in skillet, cook half the sliced onions, carrots, and parsnips, stirring often, until onions are transparent and carrots and parsnips have softened, about 10 minutes. With slotted spoon, transfer to Dutch oven. Cook remaining half of vegetables in reserved oil from skillet; transfer to Dutch oven.
4. Prepare bouquet garni: Place bay leaf, thyme, parsley, and peppercorns on square of cheesecloth; tie with kitchen twine; add to Dutch oven. Pour water into Dutch oven to barely cover meat, about 2 quarts. Bring to a boil; reduce heat, and gently simmer, partly covered, until beef is tender, about 2½ hours.
5. Meanwhile, place potatoes in medium saucepan, cover with salted water, and bring to a boil over high heat. Reduce heat; simmer, uncovered, until tender. Warm cream in small

pan over medium heat. Drain potatoes; when cool enough to handle, press through ricer into medium bowl. Stir with wooden spoon until smooth, 1 to 2 minutes. Cut 1 stick butter into chunks; add to potatoes, and whisk to incorporate. Drizzle in hot cream, whisking constantly. Whisk in 2 teaspoons salt, $1/2$ teaspoon pepper, and the nutmeg. Set aside.

6. In large skillet over medium-high heat, melt 2 tablespoons butter; add pearl onions, and sauté until golden, about 10 minutes. Remove from heat; add to Dutch oven. Return skillet to heat; add remaining 2 tablespoons butter, and melt. Add mushrooms; cook just until mushrooms release liquid, 3 to 4 minutes. Transfer to Dutch oven. Continue to simmer stew until beef is very tender and pearl onions are soft, about 30 minutes more.

7. Remove bouquet garni; discard.

8. Heat oven to 475°. Spoon stew into ovenproof ramekins about 5 inches wide and 3 inches tall. Top each with large spoonful, about 1 cup, reserved mashed potatoes. Garnish each with oregano sprig. Place ramekins on baking sheet; bake until crust is golden, about 15 minutes.

Wild-Mushroom and Spinach Lasagna

SERVES 10 TO 12

    5   pounds fresh spinach, stems removed
    1   cup (2 sticks) unsalted butter
    3   cloves garlic, peeled and finely sliced
    1   pound ricotta cheese
    6   teaspoons salt
  1¾   teaspoons freshly ground pepper
    3   pounds wild mushrooms (chanterelle,
        oyster, and shiitake), trimmed, cut
        into 1-inch pieces
   ¾   cup Madeira wine
   ½   cup chopped fresh flat-leaf parsley
  4½   cups milk
   ½   cup all-purpose flour
   ½   teaspoon nutmeg
    1   cup grated Pecorino Romano cheese
        (see the Guide)
    1   one-pound package fresh spinach
        lasagna sheets

1. Wash spinach leaves well in three changes of cold water; shake dry. Melt 1 tablespoon butter in large pan over medium heat. Add half the garlic; sauté until light golden, about 2 minutes. Add half the spinach leaves, cover, and cook, stirring occasionally, until wilted, 4 to 5 minutes. Drain spinach in a colander. Repeat with another tablespoon butter and remaining garlic and spinach. When spinach is cool enough to handle, squeeze to rid it of liquid. Roughly chop spinach; place in medium bowl. Add ricotta, 2 teaspoons salt, and 1 teaspoon pepper; mix well.

2. Melt 2 tablespoons butter in a large skillet over medium heat. Add a third of the mushrooms; season with 1 teaspoon salt and $1/4$ teaspoon pepper. Sauté until mushrooms are softened and browned, about 10 minutes. Deglaze skillet by pouring $1/4$ cup Madeira into hot skillet with mushrooms and using a wooden spoon to loosen bits cooked onto skillet. Cook mushrooms until liquid has almost evaporated. Transfer cooked mushrooms to medium bowl. Repeat with another 2 tablespoons of butter, another third of the mushrooms, and $1/4$ cup Madeira. (Reserve the final third of mushrooms and Madeira for topping.) Add two-thirds of the chopped parsley to bowl with cooked mushrooms; stir.

3. In medium saucepan over medium heat, heat 4 cups milk. Melt 8 tablespoons butter in medium saucepan over medium heat. When butter bubbles, add flour; cook, stirring constantly, 1 minute. Slowly add warmed milk; cook, whisking constantly, until mixture bubbles and becomes thick. Remove pan from heat. Stir in 2 teaspoons salt, $1/4$ teaspoon pepper, the nutmeg, and $1/2$ cup grated cheese.

4. Heat oven to 350°. Set aside $1/2$ cup sauce. Assemble lasagna: Spread $1/2$ cup sauce in bottom of 9-by-13-inch baking pan. Place layer of lasagna sheets in pan, trimming to fit; spread 1 cup spinach mixture, 1 cup mushroom mixture, and $1/2$ cup sauce on top of lasagna sheets. Repeat layers several times. For last layer, place a layer of lasagna sheets on top; spread $1/2$ cup sauce over lasagna sheets. Sprinkle with $1/2$ cup grated cheese. Bake lasagna until top is golden brown, 1 to 1¼ hours. Let stand 20 minutes before serving.

5. Just before serving, melt remaining 2 tablespoons butter in the skillet over medium heat. Add remaining third of the uncooked mushrooms; season with 1 teaspoon salt and $1/4$ teaspoon pepper. Cook until golden and tender, about 10 minutes. Deglaze skillet, with mushrooms in it, with the remaining $1/4$ cup Madeira. Stir in the remaining fresh parsley.

6. In a small saucepan, combine reserved $1/2$ cup sauce with remaining $1/2$ cup milk. Over medium heat, whisk until warm and smooth. Spoon cooked mushrooms over each serving or serve on the side. Serve lasagna with warmed sauce.

Camembert Stuffed With Pears and Walnuts

SERVES 10 TO 12

It's important the cheese is cold so it can be sliced; the glaze will warm it when poured on top.

    1   eight-ounce wheel Camembert
        or Brie cheese, cold
    1   tablespoon unsalted butter
    1   large Bosc pear, peeled and cut
        into ¼-inch dice
    2   tablespoons brandy
    1   teaspoon chopped fresh rosemary,
        plus more for garnish
    2   tablespoons balsamic vinegar
    1   tablespoon honey
    8   walnut halves

1. Slice cheese wheel in half crosswise; set aside. In a medium skillet over medium heat, melt the butter. Add the diced pear; cook until tender, about 3 minutes. Stir in the brandy, and cook 1 minute more. Add rosemary, and stir to combine. Remove from heat, and spread over bottom half of reserved sliced cheese wheel, reserving 2 tablespoons of the mixture for garnish. Transfer cheese to serving plate.

2. Return skillet to stove, and heat the balsamic vinegar and honey until simmering. Simmer mixture until slightly thickened, about 3 minutes. Set aside to cool, about 5 minutes. Pour half the glaze over cheese and reserved pear mixture; top with remaining half of cheese wheel and pears. Drizzle with remaining glaze, and garnish with walnut halves and rosemary. Serve immediately.

Pear Tart

MAKES ONE 10-INCH TART

This rustic pear tart is made in a cake pan that is 2 inches deep and 10 inches round. The base of a 10-inch tart pan is used to shape and chill the dough for the top of the tart.

- 1½ cups sugar
- 2 cinnamon sticks
- ½ teaspoon ground cinnamon
- 2 whole cloves
- 10 Anjou pears (about 5½ pounds), peeled and cut into one-inch pieces
- ¼ cup finely chopped crystallized ginger
- 1 cup (2 sticks) unsalted butter, plus more for pan
- 1½ tablespoons pure vanilla extract
- 4 whole egg yolks, plus one whole egg for glaze
- 2¾ cups all-purpose flour
- ⅛ teaspoon salt

1. Combine ½ cup sugar, cinnamon sticks, ground cinnamon, cloves, and 3 cups water in a large saucepan; bring to a simmer over medium heat. Allow to simmer until sugar has dissolved, about 5 minutes. Add the pears, cover and simmer, stirring occasionally until pears are very tender and falling apart, about 25 minutes. Remove lid; simmer, stirring frequently, until all liquid has evaporated, 30 to 40 minutes. Remove from heat, and place in a medium bowl; stir in crystallized ginger. Let cool. Remove cinnamon sticks.

2. Heat oven to 350°. Butter bottom of 10-by-2-inch-round cake pan. Cut parchment to fit bottom of pan; place in pan. Set aside. In bowl of electric mixer fitted with paddle attachment, cream butter and remaining one cup sugar until light. Add vanilla and the egg yolks, one at a time, beating well after each addition. Add flour and salt; beat just until combined (do not over beat). Divide dough in half. Place half the dough in the pan. Wrap remaining half in plastic; chill.

3. With fingers, spread dough evenly over bottom and about 1½ inches up sides of pan, sprinkling lightly with flour if dough becomes too sticky. Spread cooled pear mixture over dough. Refrigerate 15 minutes.

4. For top crust, flour a 10-inch tart-pan bottom. Press remaining dough evenly on pan bottom to make a thick, even disk; chill 15 minutes. Slide spatula between dough and pan bottom to separate; slide disk of dough over filling and press into place, making sure edges of top crust meet sides of bottom crust. Smooth top crust with small offset spatula.

5. Whisk egg in small bowl; brush onto dough. With a fork, score top of tart in lattice pattern; brush again with egg. Bake until golden brown, about 50 minutes.

6. Let tart cool in pan on wire rack, until just warm. Invert to remove from pan; turn right-side up to serve.

Caramelized Lemon Tart

MAKES ONE 12-INCH TART

- 2 cups sugar
- 1 cup freshly squeezed lemon juice, strained
- 12 large egg yolks
    Grated zest of 2 lemons
- 1 cup (2 sticks) unsalted butter, cut into pieces
- 1 twelve-inch Pâte Sucrée tart shell (recipe follows), baked and cooled
- 3 tablespoons sugar

1. Place sugar and lemon juice in large bowl. Push egg yolks through a sieve into the bowl; whisk to combine.

2. Set bowl over a pot of simmering water; whisk until mixture thickens, 15 to 20 minutes. Cook 5 minutes longer, continuing to whisk.

3. Remove bowl from heat, and stir in the zest. Stir in butter, piece by piece, until completely melted. Pour mixture into cooled tart shell. Chill until firm, at least 1 hour.

4. Preheat broiler. Remove outer ring from tart pan, and place pan on a large cookie sheet. Place outer ring upside down on top to protect pastry from burning.

5. Sift sugar evenly over top of tart, and place under broiler. Watch carefully; remove tart when top is evenly browned. Serve.

Pâte Sucrée

MAKES ONE 12-INCH TART SHELL

The addition of sugar and two egg yolks creates a sweet, slightly crunchy crust that is wonderfully suited to tarts.

- 2½ cups all-purpose flour
    Pinch of salt (optional)
- 3 tablespoons sugar
- 1 cup (2 sticks) cold unsalted butter, cut into pieces
- ¼ cup ice water
- 2 large egg yolks, beaten

1. Combine flour, salt (if using), and sugar in a medium bowl. Cut in butter with a pastry blender until mixture resembles coarse meal.

2. Beat together water and egg yolks, and drizzle into flour-butter mixture while stirring with a fork. As soon as pastry starts to hold together, stop adding liquid. Shape dough into a flat round, wrap in plastic, and chill for at least 1 hour or overnight.

3. Heat oven to 375°. Remove dough from refrigerator. On a lightly floured surface, roll out to ⅛-inch thick. Press pastry into bottom and sides of tart pan. Run a rolling pin across top to trim. (Scraps can be wrapped in plastic and frozen for later use.) Carefully line pastry with aluminum foil, and weight with beans, rice, or pastry weights. Bake for 10 to 15 minutes. When pastry begins to color around edges, remove weights and foil, and continue to bake until pastry turns golden, 10 to 12 minutes more. Place pan on a wire rack; let cool completely before filling.

Apricot Lattice Cookies

MAKES 4 DOZEN BARS OR 2 DOZEN SQUARES

3½ cups all-purpose flour
½ teaspoon salt
1⅓ cups yellow cornmeal
2¼ cups (4½ sticks) unsalted butter, room temperature
1½ cups sugar
3 large eggs, room temperature
2¼ cups apricot jam, room temperature

1. Heat oven to 375°. Whisk together flour, salt, and cornmeal. In the bowl of an electric mixer fitted with the paddle attachment, beat butter and sugar on medium speed until light and fluffy. Add eggs one at a time, beating after each addition. Reduce speed to low, and add flour mixture. Combine thoroughly.
2. Line an 11-by-17-inch baking pan with parchment. Press half the dough evenly into bottom of pan. Place another piece of parchment over dough; rub the bottom of a spoon over parchment to get dough completely smooth; remove parchment. Using an offset spatula, spread jam on dough in an even layer.
3. Fit a pastry bag (see the Guide) with #11 plain tip. Fill pastry bag with remaining dough. Pipe parallel lines of dough spaced ½ inch apart over jam. Pipe perpendicular lines spaced ½ inch apart over first lines. Bake until golden, about 30 minutes. Transfer to a wire rack to cool. Cut into about forty-eight 1½-by-3-inch bars, or about twenty-four 3-inch squares.

Caramel for Cookies

MAKES 4½ CUPS

This recipe is used for Golden Popcorn Squares, Congo Bars, and Pecan-Caramel Shortbread, and can easily be halved or doubled.

6 cups sugar
½ teaspoon cream of tartar
¼ teaspoon salt
½ cup heavy cream

Combine sugar, cream of tartar, salt, and ⅔ cup water in a wide, heavy-bottomed saucepan, with sides at least 3 inches high. Place over high heat. Let cook, without stirring, until some sugar begins to melt and turn golden, 2 to 5 minutes. Occasionally wash down sides of pan with a wet pastry brush to prevent crystals from forming. Turn heat to medium; continue to cook, stirring occasionally, until all sugar is melted, deep golden, and a candy thermometer reads 300° (hard-crack stage). While stirring, pour the cream slowly down the side of the pan. When cream is incorporated, remove from heat; transfer to a heat-proof bowl. Use right away.

Rugelach Fingers

MAKES ABOUT 5 DOZEN

These cookies use the traditional ingredients of the crescent-shaped rugelach but have a different shape.

1 cup walnuts
¾ cup (1½ sticks) cold unsalted butter, cut into ½-inch pieces, plus 3 tablespoons melted for filling
8 ounces cream cheese
2 cups all-purpose flour
½ teaspoon salt
6 ounces roughly chopped bittersweet chocolate (see the Guide)
½ cup granulated sugar
1 tablespoon ground cinnamon
¾ cup currants (see the Guide)
    Grated rind of 1 orange
3 tablespoons light corn syrup
1 large egg yolk
3 tablespoons fine sanding sugar (see the Guide), or granulated sugar

1. Heat oven to 350°. Spread walnuts on a baking pan, and bake until golden and fragrant, 10 to 15 minutes. Transfer to a wire rack to cool.
2. Place 1½ sticks butter and the cream cheese in the bowl of an electric mixer fitted with the paddle attachment. Mix on low speed until the cream cheese is broken down, but butter is still chunky. On low speed, add flour and salt, and mix until crumbly and just beginning to hold together, about 20 seconds. There should still be some small pieces of butter visible. Divide dough into two equal parts. Form each part into a flat disk, and wrap in plastic wrap. Transfer to the refrigerator to chill for 5 hours or overnight.
3. Place the chocolate in the bowl of a food processor. Pulse until the chocolate is very finely chopped, about 7 seconds. Transfer to a large bowl. Finely chop toasted walnuts by hand, and add to bowl. Add sugar, cinnamon, currants, orange rind, corn syrup, and melted butter, and combine by hand. Beat egg yolk with 1 tablespoon water, and set aside.
4. Line a 9-by-13-inch baking pan with parchment paper. Place one disk of dough between two 9-by-13-inch pieces of wax paper; roll dough into a rectangle the size of the baking pan. Line prepared baking pan with dough. Spread dough evenly with walnut mixture. Roll remaining disk of dough into a rectangle the size of the baking pan; place on top. Trim the edges of the dough so they are even. Brush the top of dough with egg-yolk mixture, and sprinkle with sugar. Bake until golden, about 35 minutes. Cool on a wire rack. Cut into fifty to sixty 2½-by-¾-inch rectangles.

Pecan-Caramel Shortbread

MAKES ABOUT 10 DOZEN

- 3½ cups pecans
- 1½ cups (3 sticks) unsalted butter
- ¾ cup packed light-brown sugar
- 2¼ cups all-purpose flour
- 1 recipe Caramel for Cookies
  (recipe, page 132)

1. Heat oven to 350°. Spread pecans on a baking pan. Bake until golden and fragrant, 10 to 15 minutes. Transfer to a wire rack to cool. Chop roughly, and set aside.
2. In the bowl of an electric mixer fitted with the paddle attachment, cream butter and sugar until light. On low speed, add flour, and mix until just combined.
3. Line an 11-by-17-inch baking pan with parchment paper. Press dough into the bottom of baking pan in an even layer. Bake until golden, about 20 minutes.
4. Using a microwave or double boiler, heat the Caramel for Cookies until liquid. Stir in the pecans, and spread mixture over the cookie layer. Return pan to oven, and bake until the caramel is slightly darkened in color, about 10 minutes. Transfer to wire rack to cool. Cut into 2¾-by-½-inch rectangles.

Golden Popcorn Squares

MAKES ABOUT 3 DOZEN

For a quicker version of these, use air-popped popcorn.

- 2 tablespoons vegetable oil, plus more for pans
- ¾ cup popping corn (enough to make 12 cups popped)
- 1½ recipes Caramel for Cookies
  (recipe, page 132)
- 2 cups salted peanuts

1. Heat oven to 350°. Brush two 9-by-13-by-2-inch baking pans with oil, line with parchment, and oil parchment. Set aside.
2. Heat oil in a large, heavy-bottomed stockpot over medium heat. When hot, add popping corn. Cover, and let cook until corn starts to pop. When the popping noises become infrequent, remove stockpot from heat.
3. Transfer popped corn to a large mixing bowl. Using a microwave or double boiler, heat caramel until liquid. Add caramel and peanuts to popcorn; toss thoroughly. Transfer mixture to one of the prepared pans, and, using the back of a wooden spoon, pack mixture as tightly as possible.
4. Bake until caramel darkens, about 20 minutes. Transfer to a wire rack to cool for 5 minutes. Using hot pads, place other prepared pan on top. Invert popcorn into second pan, and transfer to a wire rack to cool. When completely cool and hard, cut into about thirty-six 1½-by-2-inch pieces.

Congo Bars

MAKES ABOUT 15 DOZEN

Cashews, hazelnuts, walnuts, almonds, or pecans are all fine substitutes for the macadamia nuts.

- 6 cups macadamia nuts (see the Guide), halved
- 1 one-pound box graham crackers
- ½ cup (1 stick) unsalted butter, melted
- 10 ounces bittersweet chocolate, finely chopped
- 1½ cups packed sweetened shredded coconut
- 1 recipe Caramel for Cookies
  (recipe, page 132)

1. Heat oven to 350°. Spread macadamia nuts on a baking sheet; bake until golden, about 10 minutes. Set baking sheet on wire rack to cool.
2. Line an 11-by-18-inch baking pan with parchment paper. Using a food processor or rolling pin, finely crush graham crackers. Place in a medium bowl. Stir in melted butter. Press mixture into the bottom of prepared baking pan in an even layer. Sprinkle the chocolate over the graham crackers. Sprinkle the coconut over the chocolate. Sprinkle the reserved nuts over the coconut.
3. Using a microwave or double boiler, heat the Caramel for Cookies until liquid. Drizzle caramel over macadamia nuts. Bake until golden, about 20 minutes. Transfer to a wire rack to cool. Cut into ¾-by-1¼-inch pieces.

Shaker Lemon Bars

MAKES ABOUT 5 DOZEN

Begin step one the day before you plan to bake these cookies.

- 2 lemons, washed and dried
- 2 cups plus ¾ cup sugar
- 1⅛ cups (2¼ sticks) cold, unsalted butter, cut into ½-inch pieces
- ½ teaspoon salt
- 3 cups all-purpose flour
- 4 large eggs, lightly beaten
  Confectioners' sugar, for sifting

1. Slice lemons as thinly as possible; remove seeds. Toss slices with 2 cups sugar; transfer mixture to a flat resealable plastic container. Place in the refrigerator overnight.
2. Place butter, salt, remaining ¾ cup sugar, and flour in the bowl of a food processor. Process until mixture is in crumbs and starts to hold together.
3. Heat oven to 400°. Line an 11-by-17-inch baking pan with parchment paper. Press dough evenly into the bottom and up the sides of the pan, making sure there are no holes. There should be at least ½-inch crust of dough going up the sides of the pan. Bake until golden brown, about 20 minutes. Transfer to a wire rack to cool completely, about 15 minutes.
4. Place lemon-sugar mixture and eggs in the bowl of a food processor. Process until lemon rinds are in ¼- to ½-inch pieces, 30 to 40 seconds. Pour mixture over cookie crust. Bake until set, 15 to 20 minutes. Cool on a wire rack. Trim ½ inch around edges of pan. Cut into about sixty 1¼-by-2-inch pieces. Sift confectioners' sugar over cookies.

THE GUIDE

COVER

Alabaster large VASE (DAL002), 6-by-9¹/₄", $62; milk-glass FLOWERPOTS, medium and small, set of 4 small (GFV007), $28; set of 3 medium (GFV008), $28; and 3-foot-tall WHITE FEATHER TREE (XFT004), $375, from Martha By Mail, 800-950-7130 or www.marthabymail.com. Farley's SPICE DROPS, GIANT JELLIES, AND FRUIT SLICES, 800-622-4726 for retailers. NONPAREIL SPRINKLES, $2.99 for 4 ounces, from NY Cake & Baking Distributor, 56 West 22nd Street, New York, NY 10010; 800-942-2539. Assorted RIBBON from Hyman Hendler & Sons, 67 West 38th Street, New York, NY 10018; 212-840-8393 (minimum order $50); and from Tinsel Trading, 47 West 38th Street, New York, NY 10018; 212-730-1030. WRAPPING PAPER from Kate's Paperie, 561 Broadway, New York, NY 10012; 888-941-9169. GARLAND from U.S. Evergreen, 805 Sixth Avenue, New York, NY 10001; 212-741-5300. Vintage polka-dot RIBBON, $1 to $5 per yard, from French General, 35 Crosby Street, New York, NY 10013; 212-343-7474.

Page 3

Red wreath CARD from Mrs. John L. Strong Fine Stationery, 699 Madison Avenue, New York, NY 10021; 212-838-3775.

Page 6

Gray V-neck SWEATER and red SWEATER from TSE Cashmere, 827 Madison Avenue, New York, NY 10021; 212-472-7790. Wool and cashmere FABRICS from B&J Fabrics, 263 West 40th Street, New York, NY 10018; 212-354-8150. 2³/₄"-wide double-faced duchess SATIN RIBBON in Christmas Red, Dusty Rose, Rhubarb, and Latte, $4.50 per yard, from Masterstroke Canada, 416-751-4193 or www.masterstroke-canada.com. Red society SATIN RIBBON and assorted VELVET RIBBON from Hyman Hendler & Sons, 67 West 38th Street, New York, NY 10018; 212-840-8393. Minimum order $50. Assorted PIPS and STAMENS from Dulken & Derrick, 12 West 21st Street, New York, NY 10010; 212-929-3614 or www.topsilks.com. Assorted STAMENS, $2 per bag, from Toho Shoji, 990 Sixth Ave, New York, NY 10018; 212-868-7465. 26-gauge BRASS WIRE, $3.75 per small spool, and 22-gauge BRASS WIRE, $11.20 per 1-pound spool, from Metalliferous, 34 West 46th Street, New York, NY 10036; 212-944-0909 or 888-944-0909. MOUSE CAT TOY from Petco, 860 Broadway, New York, NY 10003; 212-358-0692 or www.petco.com. ASSORTED PINECONES from Winter Woods, 701 Winter Woods, Glidden, WI

54527; 715-264-4892. GLASSINE PAPER, 36¢ a sheet for 24-by-36" size, from New York Central Art Supply, 62 Third Avenue, New York, NY 10003; 212-473-7705 or 800-950-6111 or www.nycentralart.com. UNCOVERED BOXES from Kate's Paperie, 561 Broadway, New York, NY 10012; 888-941-9169. ASSORTED PAPERS from New York Central Art Supply, 62 Third Avenue, New York, NY 10003; 212-473-7705 or 800-950-6111 or www.nycentralart.com; and from Kate's Paperie, 561 Broadway, New York, NY 10012; 888-941-9169. 1" double-face SATIN ASSORTED RIBBON, $2.94 per yard, from Mokuba, 55 West 39th Street, New York, NY 10018; 212-869-8900 or www.ribbtrim.com; and from Hyman Hendler & Sons, 67 West 38th Street, New York, NY 10018; 212-840-8393. Minimum order $50. PUNCH BOWL, from Dean & DeLuca; 800-999-0306 or www.deandeluca.com. Farley's SPICE DROPS, GIANT JELLIES, AND FRUIT SLICES, 800-622-4726 for retailers. Starburst fruit twists, 800-551-0683 for retailers or www.starburst.com. STYROFOAM CONES from Michael's craft stores, 800-642-4235 or www.michaels.com for nearest location.

Page 7

ASSORTED RIBBON from Hyman Hendler & Sons, 67 West 38th Street, New York, NY 10018; 212-840-8393 (minimum order $50); and from Tinsel Trading, 47 West 38th Street, New York, NY 10018; 212-730-1030. WRAPPING PAPER from Kate's Paperie, 561 Broadway, New York, NY 10012; 888-941-9169. William IV cut-glass COMPOTES from James II Galleries, 11 East 57th Street, Fourth Floor, New York, NY 10022; 212-355-7040 or www.james2.com. LAMETTA TEARDROP LOOPS (#R594S), $5 per pair, and ANGEL'S-HAIR TINSEL (#J925S), $3.50 a box, from D. Blumchen & Co., P.O. Box 1210, Ridgewood, NJ 07451; 201-652-5595.

Page 9

3-foot-tall WHITE FEATHER TREE (XFT004), $375, from Martha By Mail, 800-950-7130 or www.marthaby mail.com. Farley's SPICE DROPS, GIANT JELLIES, AND FRUIT SLICES, 800-622-4726 for retailers. NON-PAREIL SPRINKLES, $2.99 for 4 ounces, from NY Cake & Baking Distributor, 56 West 22nd Street New York, NY 10010; 800-942-2539. ASSORTED RIBBON from Hyman Hendler & Sons, 67 West 38th Street, New York, NY 10018; 212-840-8393 (minimum order $50); and from Tinsel Trading, 47 West 38th Street, New York, NY 10018; 212-730-1030. WRAPPING PAPER from Kate's Paperie, 561 Broadway, New York, NY 10012; 888-941-9169. GARLAND from U.S. Evergreen, 805 Sixth Avenue, New York, NY 10001; 212-741-5300.

TRIMMING THE TREE IN TENNESSEE

Pages 12 to 21

ANTIQUE MATTRESS TICKING and VINTAGE LINENS from Laval Antique Collections, 4092 East Brookhaven Drive, Atlanta, GA 30319; 404-237-7389. ASSORTED ANTIQUES from Green Hills Antique Mall, 4108 Hillsboro Road, Nashville, TN 37215; 615-383-9851 or www.greenhillsantiques.com; and from Scott Antique Market, 3650 Jonesboro Road, Atlanta, GA 30354; 404-361-2000, held the second weekend of each month. CHRISTMAS TREE from Hewitt Garden and Design Center, 2525 Hillsboro Road, Franklin, TN 37069; 615-661-6767. ASSORTED GREENS AND FLOWERS from Import Flowers, 3636 Murphy Road, Nashville, TN 37209; 615-297-0397. DRIED TALLOW BERRIES, $3 per 3-ounce bunch, from Galveston Wreath Co., 1124 25th Street Galveston, TX 77550; 409765-8597. RIBBON WREATHS from Aix, 462 Broome Street, New York, NY 10013; 212-941-7919. 28-gauge NICKEL WIRE, $3.25 for 40 yards, from Toho Shoji, 990 Sixth Avenue, New York, NY 10018; 212-868-7465. 3" LAMETTA BUMPS (#J559S), $10 for 2m, from D.Blumchen & Co., P.O. Box 1210H, Ridgewood, NJ 07451; 201-652-5595. Le Creuset TERRINE (#CLPT), $95; 9-piece PASTRY-CUTTER SET (ABMD-53B), $15; fluted TARTLET MOLD with removable bottom (#ATTLBS-4), $2.95; various PUDDING MOLDS; and 12-cup nonstick TUBE BAKING PAN (#BBNT-NS-12), $29.95, from Bridge Kitchenware, 214 East 52nd Street, New York, NY 10022; 212-838-1901 or www.bridgekitchenware.com. Flex 10" PASTRY BAG, $2.99; #11 PASTRY TIP, $1.99; FINE SANDING SUGAR, $2.99 per 4-ounce package; Flex 12" PASTRY BAG, $3.99; PASTRY TIP, $2.59; and ANGEL COOKIE CUTTERS, $2, from NY Cake & Baking Distributor, 56 West 22nd Street, New York, NY 10010; 800-942-2539.

Page 17

MERCURY-GLASS BEADS, $10 a strand, from French General, 35 Crosby Street, New York, NY 10013; 212-343-7474.

CANDY PARTY WITH KIDS

Pages 22 to 31

Milk-glass FLOWERPOTS, medium and small, set of 4 small (GFV007), $28; set of 3 medium (GFV008), $28; GARDEN CLOGS (AGC002), $39; and 3-foot-tall WHITE FEATHER TREE (XFT004), $375, from Martha By Mail, 800-950-7130 or www.marthabymail.com. Farley's SPICE DROPS, GIANT JELLIES, AND FRUIT SLICES, 800-622-4726 for retailers. Starburst FRUIT TWISTS, 800-551-0683 or www.starburst.com for retailers. Vintage polka-dot RIBBON, $1 to $5 per yard, from French General, 35 Crosby Street, New York, NY 10013; 212-343-7474. NONPAREIL SPRINKLES, $2.99 for 4 ounces, from NY Cake & Baking Distributor, 56 West 22nd Street New York, NY 10010; 800-942-2539. STYROFOAM BALLS AND CONES, from Michael's craft stores; 800-642-4235 or www.michaels.com for nearest location. Mini PEPPERMINT PILLOWS AND STICK CANDY, from Hammond's Candy, 4969 Colorado Blvd., Denver, CO 80216; 888-226-3999. Various holiday COOKIE CUTTERS from Bridge Kitchenware, 214 East 52nd Street, New York, NY 10022; 212-838-1901 or www.bridgekitchenware.com; also from NY Cake & Baking Distributor, 56 West 22nd Street New York, NY 10010; 800-942-2539. 26-gauge NICKEL WIRE, $4.50 per mini spool, $20.10 per 1-pound spool; from Metalliferous, 34 West 46th Street, New York, NY 10036; 212-944-0909 or 888-944-0909. 4-ply WAXED LINEN TWINE, $8.50 per spool, from Caning Shop, 926 Gilman Street, Berkeley, CA 94710; 800-544-3373.

CHRISTMAS EVE IN MAINE

Page 32

RIBBON from Hyman Hendler & Sons, 67 West 38th Street, New York, NY 10018; 212-840-8393. Minimum order $50. Orsini FABRIC (#5187) from Fortuny Fabrics, 979 Third Avenue, Suite 1632, New York, NY 10022; 212-753-7153 for retailers. ASSORTED PINECONES from Winter Woods, 701 Winter Woods, Glidden, WI 54527; 715-264-4892 or www.winter-woods.com. HARNESS SET, $7.95 per stand; PLUGS, 99¢ each; 6-WATT BULBS, $1.49 for pack of two, from Rosetta Lighting & Supply Co., 21 West 46th Street, New York, NY 10036; 212-719-4381.

Page 33

PAJAMAS from Space Kiddets, 46 East 21st Street, New York, NY 10010; 212-420-9878.

Page 35

ASSORTED PINECONES from Winter Woods, 701 Winter Woods, Glidden, WI 54527; 715-264-4892 or www.winterwoods.com. 22-gauge BRASS WIRE, $11.20 per small spool, from Metalliferous, 34 West 46th Street, New York, NY 10036; 212-944-0909 or 888-944-0909. Beige cabled SWEATER from TSE Cashmere, 827 Madison Avenue, New York, NY 10021; 212-472-7790.

Page 36

RIBBON from Hyman Hendler & Sons, 67 West 38th Street, New York, NY 10018; 212-840-8393. Minimum order $50. Red wreath PLACE CARD from Mrs. John L. Strong Fine Stationery, 699 Madison Avenue, New York, NY 10021; 212-838-3775. Black V-neck SWEATER and red SHIRT from Paul Smith, 108 Fifth Avenue, New York, NY 10011; 212-627-9770. Plaid SHIRT from Banana Republic; 888-906-2800 or www.bananarepublic.com. Gray V-neck SWEATER and red SWEATER from TSE Cashmere, 827 Madison Avenue, New York, NY 10021; 212-472-7790.

Page 37

Lucrezia driftwood monotone FABRIC (#5284) from Fortuny Fabrics, 979 Third Avenue, Suite 1632, New York, NY 10022; 212-753-7153 for retailers.

Page 38

William IV cut-glass COMPOTES from James II Galleries, 11 East 57th Street, Fourth Floor, New York, NY 10022; 212-355-7040 or www.james2.com.

Page 40

Black V-neck SWEATER, RED SHIRT, BLACK PANTS, AND GRAY PANTS all from Paul Smith, 108 Fifth Avenue, New York, NY 10011; 212-627-9770. Plaid SHIRT from Banana Republic; 888-906-2800 or www.bananarepublic.com. Gray V-neck SWEATER and red SWEATER from TSE Cashmere, 827 Madison Avenue, New York, NY 10021; 212-472-7790. Black PANTS from Chaiken and Capone, available at Barneys or 212-826-8900 or 800-777-0087 for retailers. Black PANTS from Prada, 212-307-9300. Dark-red SWEATER from J.Crew, 800-562-0258 or www.jcrew.com.

Page 41

9 1/2" KUGELHOPF PAN, $24.99, from NY Cake & Baking Distributor, 56 West 22nd Street, New York, NY 10010; 800-942-2539. SILPAT nonstick baking mat (KSP001 and KSP002), $38 for 16 1/2-by-24 1/4" mat, $24 for 11 5/8-by-16 1/2" mat, from Martha By Mail, 800-950-7130 or www.marthabymail.com.

CHRISTMAS DINNER IN MANHATTAN

Page 42

GARLAND from U.S. Evergreen, 805 Sixth Avenue, New York, NY 10001; 212-741-5300. Antique sterling Christofle FLATWARE, $2,100, from Clary & Co., 372 Bleecker Street, New York, NY 10014; 212-229-1773. Antique French DINING TABLE AND CHAIRS from Pierre Deux Antiques, 369 Bleecker Street, New York, NY 10014; 212-243-7740.

Page 43

Assorted RIBBON from Hyman Hendler & Sons, 67 West 38th Street, New York, NY 10018; 212-840-8393 (minimum order $50); and from Tinsel Trading, 47 West 38th Street, New York, NY 10018; 212-730-1030. WRAPPING PAPER from Kate's Paperie, 561 Broadway, New York, NY 10012; 888-941-9169.

Page 44

Antique French CHAMPAGNE FLUTES from Pierre Deux Antiques, 369 Bleecker Street, New York, NY 10014; 212-243-7740. 2³/₄"-wide double-faced duchess SATIN RIBBON in Christmas Red, Dusty Rose, Rhubarb, and Latte, $4.50 per yard, from Masterstroke Canada, 416-751-4193 or www.masterstroke-canada.com. Red society SATIN RIBBON AND ASSORTED VELVET RIBBONS from Hyman Hendler & Sons, 67 West 38th Street, New York, NY 10018; 212-840-8393. Minimum order $50. Assorted PIPS AND STAMENS from Dulken & Derrick, 12 West 21st Street, New York, NY 10010; 212-929-3614 or www.topsilks.com. ASSORTED STAMENS, $2 per bag, from Toho Shoji, 990 Sixth Ave, New York, NY 10018; 212-868-7465. 26-gauge BRASS WIRE, $3.75 per small spool, from Metalliferous, 34th West 46th Street, New York, NY 10036; 212-944-0909 or 888-944-0909. 19" STYRO-FOAM WREATH from B&J Florists Supply, 103 West 28th Street, New York, NY 10001, 212-564-6086.

Page 45

Wool and cashmere FABRICS from B&J Fabrics, 263 West 40th Street, New York, NY 10018; 212-354-8150. 2³/₄"-wide double-faced duchess SATIN RIBBON in Christmas Red, Dusty Rose, Rhubarb, and Latte, $4.50 per yard, from Masterstroke Canada, 416-751-4193 or www.masterstroke.com. Red society SATIN RIBBON AND ASSORTED VELVET RIBBONS

from Hyman Hendler & Sons, 67 West 38th Street, New York, NY 10018; 212-840-8393. Minimum order $50. ASSORTED PIPS AND STAMENS from Dulken & Derrick, 12 West 21st Street, New York, NY 10010; 212-929-3614 or www.topsilks.com. ASSORTED STAMENS, $2 per bag, from Toho Shoji, 990 Sixth Avenue, New York, NY 10018; 212-868-7465. 26-gauge BRASS WIRE, $3.75 per small spool, from Metalliferous, 34th West 46th Street, New York, NY 10036; 212-944-0909 or 888-944-0909. Mouse CAT TOY from Petco, 860 Broadway, New York, NY 10003; 212-358-0692 or www.petco.com.

Page 46

12-by-18-by-1" JELLY-ROLL PAN (ABJR-2), $17.95, from Bridge Kitchenware, 214 East 52nd Street, New York, NY 10022; 212-838-1901 or www.bridgekitchenware.com.

Page 47

Antique clear etched 18th-century French WINE GOBLETS from Pierre Deux Antiques, 369 Bleecker Street, New York, NY 10014; 212-243-7740.

OPEN HOUSE ON NEW YEAR'S DAY

Page 50

PUNCH BOWL from Dean & DeLuca; 800-999-0306 or www.deandeluca.com.

Page 55

Assorted ORIGAMI PAPER AND METALLIC PENS from New York Central Art Supply, 62 Third Avenue, New York, NY 10003; 212-473-7705 or 800-950-6111 or www.nycentralart.com.

Page 57

10-by-2" round CAKE PAN (ABRC-102), from Bridge Kitchenware, 214 East 52nd Street, New York, NY 10022; 212-838-1901 or www.bridgekitchenware.com; and from NY Cake & Baking Distributor, 56 West 22nd Street, New York, NY 10010; 800-942-2539.

Page 58

Special thanks to: Stefanie Lynen. GLASSINE PAPER, 36¢ a sheet for 24-by-36" size, from New York Central Art Supply, 62 Third Avenue, New York, NY 10003; 212-473-7705 or 800-950-6111 or www.nycentralart.com. UNCOVERED BOXES from Kate's Paperie, 561 Broadway, New York, NY 10012; 888-941-9169. ASSORTED PAPERS from New York Central Art Supply, 62 Third Avenue, New York, NY 10003; 212-473-7705 or 800-950-6111 or www.nycentralart.com; and from Kate's Paperie, 561 Broadway, New York, NY 10012; 888-941-9169. 1" double face assorted SATIN

RIBBON, $2.94 per yard, from Mokuba, 55 West 39th Street, New York, NY 10018; 212-869-8900 or www.ribbtrim.com; and from Hyman Hendler & Sons, 67 West 38th Street, New York, NY 10018; 212-840-8393. Minimum order $50.

Page 59

UNCOVERED BOXES from Kate's Paperie, 561 Broadway, New York, NY 10012; 888-941-9169. ASSORTED PAPERS from New York Central Art Supply, see above, and from Kate's Paperie, see above. 1" double face assorted SATIN RIBBON, $2.94 per yard, from Mokuba, 55 West 39th Street, New York, NY 10018; 212-869-8900 or www.ribbtrim.com; and from Hyman Hendler & Sons, 67 West 38th Street, New York, NY 10018; 212-840-8393. Minimum order $50.

Page 60

3-foot-tall WHITE FEATHER TREE (XFT004), $375, from Martha By Mail, 800-950-7130 or www.marthaby-mail.com. Farley's SPICE DROPS, GIANT JELLIES, AND FRUIT SLICES, 800-622-4726 for retailers. NON-PAREIL SPRINKLES, $2.99 for 4 ounces, from NY Cake & Baking Distributor, 56 West 22nd Street New York, NY 10010; 800-942-2539.

Page 61

ASSORTED RIBBON from French General, 35 Crosby Street, New York, NY 10013; 212-343-7474. 1/4" VINTAGE SILVER RIBBON, $3 per yard, and VINTAGE SILVER RICKRACK, from Tinsel Trading, 47 West 38th Street, New York, NY 10018; 212-730-1030. ASSORTED WRAPPING PAPER from Kate's Paperie, 561 Broadway, New York, NY 10012; 888-941-9169.

TINSEL AND COOKIE ORNAMENTS

Page 63

LAMETTA TEARDROP LOOPS (#R594S), $5 per pair, and ANGEL'S-HAIR TINSEL (#J925S), $3.50 a box, from D. Blumchen & Co., P.O. Box 1210, Ridgewood, NJ 07451; 201-652-5595.

Page 64

28-gauge NICKEL WIRE, $3.25 for 40 yards, from Toho Shoji, 990 Sixth Avenue, New York, NY 10018; 212-868-7465.

Page 65

28-gauge NICKEL WIRE, $3.25 per 40 yards, from Toho Shoji, 990 Sixth Avenue, New York, NY 10018; 212-868-7465. 3" LAMETTA BUMPS (#J559S), $10 for 2m, from D. Blumchen and Co., P.O. Box 1210, Ridgewood, NJ 07451; 201-652-5595.

Page 67

ANTIQUE WALLPAPER from Secondhand Rose, 138 Duane Street, New York, NY 10013; 212-393-9002 or www.secondhandrose.com. MATTRESS TICKING (#1

in Mustard), $35 per yard, from Coconut Company, 131 Greene Street, New York, NY 10012; 212-539-1940. "Rose Garden" FABRIC, $32 per yard, from ABC Carpet & Home, 888 Broadway, New York, NY 10003; 212-473-3000 or www.abchome.com. "Mistletoe" striped FABRIC, $165 per yard, from Bennison Fabrics, 76 Greene Street, New York, NY 10012; 212-941-1212.

Page 68

3" LAMETTA BUMPS (#J559S), $10 for 2m, and WIDE LAMETTA (#J922S), $10 for 6 1/2 feet, from D. Blumchen and Co., P.O. Box 1210, Ridgewood, NJ 07451; 201-652-5595. BELLS from Toho Shoji, 990 Sixth Avenue, New York, NY 10018; 212-868-7465.

Page 69

MERINGUE POWDER (#MP10), $9.99 per 10-ounce package; LARGE COUPLER, $3.99; 10" PASTRY BAG, $2.99; GEL PASTE, $2.49; and FOOD COLORING, $2.49, from NY Cake & Baking Distributor, 56 West 22nd Street, New York, NY 10010; 800-942-2539.

DECORATING WITH CANDY

Pages 70 to 75

Milk-glass FLOWERPOTS, medium and small, set of 4 small (GFV007), $28; set of 3 medium (GFV008), $28; GARDEN CLOGS (AGC002), $39; and 3-foot-tall WHITE FEATHER TREE (XFT004), $375, from Martha By Mail, 800-950-7130 or www.marthabymail.com. Farley's SPICE DROPS, GIANT JELLIES, AND FRUIT SLICES, 800-622-4726 for retailers. Starburst FRUIT TWISTS, call 800-551-0683 for retailers or www.starburst.com. Vintage polka-dot RIBBON, $1 to $5 per yard, from French General, 35 Crosby Street, New York, NY 10013; 212-343-7474. NONPAREIL SPRINKLES, from NY Cake & Baking Distributor, 56 West 22nd Street New York, NY 10010; 800-942-2539. STYROFOAM BALLS AND CONES from Michael's craft stores, 800-642-4235 for nearest location or www.michaels.com. Mini PEPPERMINT PILLOWS AND STICK CANDY from Hammond's Candy, 4969 Colorado Blvd., Denver, CO 80216; 303-455-2320 or 888-226-3999. Various holiday COOKIE CUTTERS from Bridge Kitchenware, 214 East 52nd Street, New York, NY 10022; 212-838-1901; and from NY Cake & Baking Distributor, 56 West 22nd Street New York, NY 10010; 800-942-2539. 26-gauge NICKEL WIRE, $4.50 per mini spool, $20.10 per 1-pound spool, from Metalliferous, 34 West 46th Street, New York, NY 10036; 212-944-0909 or 888-944-0909. 4-ply WAXED LINEN TWINE, $8.50 per spool from Caning Shop, 926 Gilman Street, Berkeley, CA 94710; 800-544-3373.

PINECONES, STOCKINGS, AND ROSES

Page 77

GOLD BEADS, assorted styles available, from M&J Trimmings, 1008 Sixth Avenue, New York, NY 10018; 212-391-9072. ASSORTED PINECONES from Winter Woods, 701 Winter Woods, Glidden, WI 54527; 715-264-4892 or www.winterwoods.com.

Page 78

ASSORTED PINECONES from Winter Woods, 701 Winter Woods, Glidden, WI 54527; 715-264-4892 or www.winterwoods.com. SILK EMBROIDERY RIBBON from YLI Corporation, 161 West Main Street, Rock Hill, SC 29730; 800-296-8139. Zynolyte GOLD SPRAY PAINT, $5, from Jamali Hardware and Garden Supplies, 149 West 28th Street, New York, NY 10001; 212-244-4025.

Page 79

ASSORTED PINECONES from Winter Woods, 701 Winter Woods, Glidden, WI 54527; 715-264-4892 or www.winterwoods.com. 22-gauge BRASS WIRE, $11.20 per small spool, from Metalliferous, 34th West 46th Street, New York, NY 10036; 212-944-0909 or 888-944-0909.

Page 80

ASSORTED PINECONES from Winter Woods, 701 Winter Woods, Glidden, WI 54527; 715-264-4892 or www.winterwoods.com. GOLD METALLIC RIBBON, $3 per yard, from Tinsel Trading, 47 West 38th Street, New York, NY 10018; 212-730-1030. GOLD WIDE LAMETTA TINSEL ROPING (J922G), $10 per 6 1/2-foot length, from D. Blumchen & Co., 162 East Ridgewood Avenue, P.O. Box 1210, Ridgewood, NJ 07451; 201-652-5595.

Page 81

OAK CHAIR with velvet cushion, $995, from ABC Carpet & Home, 888 Broadway, New York, NY 10003; 212-473-3000 or www.abchome.com.

Page 82

1/4" ARTIST'S TAPE, $4.25, from New York Central Art Supply, 62 Third Avenue, New York, NY 10003;

800-950-6111. Victorian ruby flash GOBLET, circa 1850, $1,575 for a pair, from James Robinson, 480 Park Avenue, New York, NY 10022; 212-752-6166. Pressed-glass COMPOTE by Dalzell-Viking, $32, from Fishs Eddy, 889 Broadway, New York, NY 10012; 877-347-4733. William IV cut-glass COMPOTES from James II Galleries, 11 East 57th Street, Fourth Floor, New York, NY 10022; 212-355-7040 or www.james2.com.

Page 83
WALNUT DUMBWAITER, $2,095, from ABC Carpet & Home, 888 Broadway, New York, NY 10003; 212-473-3000 or www.abchome.com.

RIBBON, LIGHT, AND GLITTER

Pages 84 and 85
2³/₄"-wide double-faced duchess SATIN RIBBON in Christmas Red, Dusty Rose, Rhubarb, and Latte, $4.50 per yard, from Masterstroke Canada, 416-751-4193 or www.masterstrokecanada.com. Red Society SATIN RIBBON AND ASSORTED VELVET RIBBONS from Hyman Hendler & Sons, 67 West 38th Street, New York, NY 10018; 212-840-8393. Minimum order $50. ASSORTED PIPS AND STAMENS from Dulken & Derrick, 12 West 21st Street, New York, NY 10010; 212-929-3614 or www.topsilks.com. ASSORTED STAMENS, $2 per bag, from Toho Shoji, 990 Sixth Avenue, New York, NY 10018; 212-868-7465. 26-gauge BRASS WIRE, $3.75 per small spool, from Metalliferous, 34 West 46th Street, New York, NY 10036; 212-944-0909 or 888-944-0909. 19" STYROFOAM WREATH from B&J Florists Supply, 103 West 28th Street, New York, NY 10001; 212-564-6086.

Page 86
2³/₄"-wide double-faced duchess SATIN RIBBON in Christmas Red, Dusty Rose, Rhubarb, and Latte, $4.50 per yard, from Masterstroke Canada, 416-751-4193 or www.masterstrokecanada.com. Red society SATIN RIBBON AND ASSORTED VELVET

RIBBONS from Hyman Hendler & Sons, 67 West 38th Street, New York, NY 10018; 212-840-8393. Minimum order $50. ASSORTED PIPS AND STAMENS from Dulken & Derrick, 12 West 21st Street, New York, NY 10010; 212-929-3614 or www.topsilks.com. ASSORTED STAMENS, $2 per bag, from Toho Shoji, 990 Sixth Ave, New York, NY 10018; 212-868-7465. 26-gauge BRASS WIRE, $3.75 per spool, from Metalliferous, 34 West 46th Street, New York, NY 10036; 212-944-0909 or 888-944-0909.

Page 88
ASSORTED RIBBON from Hyman Hendler & Sons, 67 West 38th Street, New York, NY 10018; 212-840-8393 (minimum order $50); and from Tinsel Trading, 47 West 38th Street, New York, NY 10018; 212-730-1030. WRAPPING PAPER from Kate's Paperie, 561 Broadway, New York, NY 10012; 888-941-9169.

Page 90
ASSORTED RIBBON from Hyman Hendler & Sons, 67 West 38th Street, New York, NY 10018; 212-840-8393 (Minimum order $50); and from Tinsel Trading, 47 West 38th Street, New York, NY 10018; 212-730-1030. WRAPPING PAPER from Kate's Paperie, 561 Broadway, New York, NY 10012; 888-941-9169. RIBBON CANDY from Hammond's Candy, 4969 Colorado Boulevard, Denver, CO 80216; 303-455-2320 or 888-226-3999.

FLOURISHES AND FAVORS

Page 92
FLORAL WIRE from B&J Florists Supply, 103 West 28th Street, New York, NY 10001; 212-564-6086.

Page 93
WIRE WREATH FORMS from Galveston Wreath Company, 1124 25th Street, Galveston, TX 77550; 409-765-8597. 28-gauge GREEN FLORAL WIRE, $1.09 for forty 18" pieces, from Dorothy Biddle Service, 348 Greeley Lake Road, Greeley, PA 18425; 570-226-3239.

Page 94
24-gauge GREEN FLORAL WIRE for wreaths, $3.75 for 354-foot spool, from Dorothy Biddle Service, 348 Greeley Lake Road, Greeley, PA 18425; 570-226-3239. WIRE WREATH FORMS; 18" WREATH FORM, $6; and 24" WREATH FORM, $7, from Galveston Wreath Company, 1124 25th Street, Galveston, TX 77550; 409-765-8597.

Page 96
3-by-3" CUBE BOXES (#L128B), $3 each from Kate's Paperie, 561 Broadway, New York, NY 10012; 888-

941-9169. ASSORTED PAPERS on boxes from New York Central Art Supply, 62 Third Avenue, New York, NY 10003; 212-473-7705 or 800-950-6111 or www.nycentralart.com. Minimum order $15. KRAFT BALLOTIN BOXES (#MB1KR), 99¢ each, from Glerup-Revere Company, P.O. Box 31419, Seattle, WA 98103; 206-545-1850, ext. 220. Minimum order 50 boxes. PLASTIC/METAL HANDLES, $14.75 for 150, and BAKER'S TWINE, $9.50 for 2-pound cone, from Wolf Paper & Twine, 680 Sixth Avenue, New York, NY 10010; 212-675-4870. FLOWERED RICKRACK, $1 per yard, from Tinsel Trading, 47 West 38th Street, New York, NY 10018; 212-730-1030. Red and khaki "cotton tie" PAPER RIBBON from Sample House, 800-626-2645 for retailers. SILVER EYELETS from Steinlauf & Stoller, 239 West 39th Street, New York, NY 10018; 877-869-0321 or www. steinlaufandstoller.com.

Page 97
Medium STAINLESS-STEEL PAN, 16-by-12-by-1¹/₂" (KRE002), $20, from Martha By Mail, 800-950-7130 or www.marthabymail.com. CELLOPHANE, $12.99 for 100-foot roll, and silver CAKE BOTTOM, assorted sizes, from NY Cake & Baking Distributor, 56 West 22nd Street, New York, NY 10010; 800-942-2539. Asahi-world BOOK CLOTH in crimson (#A 0122), $12 per yard, from Talas, 568 Broadway, New York, NY 10012; 212-219-0770 or www.talas-nyc.com.

Page 99
Assorted ORIGAMI PAPER AND METALLIC PENS from New York Central Art Supply, 62 Third Avenue, New York, NY 10003; 212-473-7705 or 800-950-6111 or www.nycentralart.com. Minimum order $15.

Page 100
Various holiday COOKIE CUTTERS from Bridge Kitchenware, 214 East 52nd Street, New York, NY 10022; 212-838-1901 or www.bridgekitchenware.com; and from NY Cake & Baking Distributor, 56 West 22nd Street New York, NY 10010; 800-942-2539.

THE RECIPES

Pages 102 to 109

FRESH TARRAGON AND THYME LEAVES from The Herb Lady, 52792 42nd Avenue, Lawrence, MI 49064; 616-674-3879. Le Crueset TERRINE (#CLPT), $95, fluted TARTLET MOLD with removable bottom (#ATTL-BS-4), $2.95; 12-cup nonstick TUBE PAN (#BBNT-NS-12), $29.95, from Bridge Kitchenware, 214 East 52nd Street, New York, NY 10022; 212-838-1901 or www.bridgekitchenware.com. SHUCKED OYSTERS, $9.99 to $15.99 per dozen (juice included, shells included upon request), from Citarella, 2135 Broadway, New York, NY 10023; 212-874-0383. Gwaltney genuine Smithfield uncooked COUNTRY-CURED HAM (#662C), $56, from Basse's Choice & Gwaltney, P.O. Box 1, Smithfield, VA 23431; 800-292-2773. Taylor CANDY THERMOMETER, $3.50 to $15.75, from Broadway Panhandler, 477 Broome Street, New York, NY 10013; 212-966-3434. Valrhona BITTERSWEET CHOCOLATE, $16.50 per pound, and SEMISWEET CHOCOLATE from Sweet Celebrations, 800-328-6722. PEARL CRYSTAL SUGAR (#1410), $3.50 per 3-pound bag, and Brown Demerara AMBER SUGAR (#1095), $2.95 per 1-pound bag, from King Arthur Flour Baker's Catalog, 800-827-6836 or www.kingarthurflour.com. FINE SANDING SUGAR, $1.99 per 4-ounce package; Flex 10" PASTRY BAG, $2.99; #11 PASTRY TIP, $1.99; FINE SANDING SUGAR, $2.99 per 4-ounce package; Flex 12" PASTRY BAG, $3.99; PASTRY TIP, $2.59; and ANGEL COOKIE CUTTERS, $2, from NY Cake & Baking Distributor, 56 West 22nd Street, New York, NY 10010; 800-942-2539. Various holiday COOKIE CUTTERS from Bridge Kitchenware, 214 East 52nd Street, New York, NY 10022; 212-838-1901 or www. bridgekitchenware.com.

Pages 112 to 119

SMOKED SEA SCALLOPS, $29 per pound, from Sullivan Harbor Farm Smokehouse, P.O. Box 96, Sullivan Harbor, ME 04664; 800-422-4014. 9$^{1}/_{2}$" KUGELHOPF PAN, $24.99, from NY Cake & Baking Distributor, 56 West 22nd Street, New York, NY 10010; 800-942-2539. SILPAT NONSTICK BAKING MAT (KSP001 and KSP002), $38 for 16$^{1}/_{2}$-by-24$^{1}/_{4}$" mat, $24 for 11$^{5}/_{8}$-by-16$^{1}/_{2}$" mat, from Martha By Mail, 800-950-7130 or www.marthabymail.com. Valrhona BITTERSWEET CHOCOLATE, $16.50 per pound, from Sweet Celebrations, 800-328-6722.

Pages 120 to 125

DRIED FIGS, $4.50 to $6.25 per pound; DRIED CURRANTS, $3.50 per pound; and DRIED PEARS, $6.25 per pound, from A.L. Bazzini Company, 800-228-0172. CRYSTALLIZED GINGER, $4.99 per 6$^{1}/_{2}$ ounces, from Royal Pacific Foods, 800-551-5284 for stores. MASCARPONE, $4.50 for 8 ounces, and Rouge GOOSE FAT, $10 per 26.6-ounce can, from Dean & DeLuca, 800-999-0306. KUMQUATS from Melissa's World Variety Produce, 800-588-0151 or www. melissas.com. MERINGUE POWDER (#MP10), $9.99 per 10-ounce package; large COUPLER, $3.99; 10" PASTRY BAG, $2.99; GEL PASTE, $2.49, and FOOD COLORING, $2.49, from NY Cake & Baking Distributor, 56 West 22nd Street, New York, NY 10010; 800-942-2539. POPOVER TINS available from Bridge Kitchenware, 214 East 52nd Street, New York, NY 10022; 212-838-1901 or www.bridgekitchenware.com.

Pages 120 to 125

SILPAT NONSTICK BAKING MAT (KSP001 and KSP002), $38 for 16$^{1}/_{2}$-by-24$^{1}/_{4}$" mat, $24 for 11$^{5}/_{8}$-by-16$^{1}/_{2}$" mat, and JAPANESE MANDOLINE (KTM 001), $68, from Martha By Mail, 800-950-7130 or www.marthabymail.com. WHOLE BLACK PEPPERCORNS, $5.49 per 8-ounce bag, from Penzey's Spices, P.O. Box 933, Muskego, WI 53150; 414-679-7207 or www.penzeys.com. JUNIPER BERRIES, 90¢ per ounce, from Dandelion Botanical Company, 708 North 34th Street, Seattle, WA 98103; 206-545-8892 or 877-778-4869. Rouge GOOSE FAT, $10 per 26.6-ounce can, from Dean & DeLuca, 800-999-0306. 8.75-quart DUTCH OVEN by Le Creuset, $239.95, from Sur La Table, 800-243-0852. PECORINO ROMANO cheese from Murray's Cheese Shop, 212-243-3289 or 888-692-4339. Flex 10" PASTRY BAG, $2.99; #11 PASTRY TIP, $1.99; Flex 12" PASTRY BAG, $3.99; and PASTRY TIP, $2.59; and FINE SANDING SUGAR, $2.99 per 4-ounce package, from NY Cake & Baking Distributor, 56 West 22nd Street, New York, NY 10010; 800-942-2539. Valrhona BITTERSWEET CHOCOLATE, $16.50 per pound, from Sweet Celebrations, 800-328-6722. DRIED CURRANTS, $3.50 per pound, and MACADAMIA NUTS, $9.25 per pound, from A.L. Bazzini Company, 800-228-0172.

CONTRIBUTORS

The creation of the annual Christmas book begins long before the first snowflake of the season falls. A special thanks to Eric A. Pike, Creative Director of Publishing and our very own Father Christmas; his passion for the holidays is evident twelve months a year. Thank you, too, to the editors, art directors, and stylists whose inspirational ideas contributed to this volume, notably, Neje Bailey, Stephana Bottom, Frances Boswell, Kerin Brooks, Claudia Bruno, Anthony Cochran, Joshua Dake, James Dunlinson, Stephen Drucker, Stephen Earle, Hosanna Houser, Joelle Hoverson, Fritz Karch, Megen Lee, Jodi Levine, Judith Lockhart, Peter Mars, Sophie Mathoulin, Jim McKeever, Hannah Milman, Melissa Morgan, Pamela Morris, Page Marchese Norman, Laura Normandin, Ayesha Patel, Claire Perez, Helen Quinn, Nikki Rooker, Kelli Ronci, Scot Schy, Wendy Sidewater, Susan Spungen, Curtis Smith, Gael Towey, Gregory Wegweiser, and to everyone at Oxmoor House, Clarkson Potter, Satellite Graphics, and R.R. Donnelley and Sons Company. Thank you to Peter Callahan and Josephine Sasso. Finally, thank you to Martha, for inspiring us to reach for the best.

PHOTOGRAPHY

WILLIAM ABRANOWICZ: 8, 134, 138

SANG AN: bookplate, 26 (left), 72, 73, 74 (top left, bottom), 75, 109

CHRISTOPHER BAKER: 12, 13, 15, 16 (top left, top right, bottom right), 18, 19 (top right, bottom left and right), 20, 21, 52, 102, 137

TODD EBERLE: 9 (top)

DANA GALLAGHER: 96 (top, bottom left), 97 (top, bottom right)

GENTL & HYERS: 3, 6 (top left, top right, middle right, bottom left), 7 (top center), 22-25, 26 (right), 27-36, 38-41, 61, 71 (bottom), 74 (top right), 76-80, 82 (bottom left), 84, 110, 112, 114, 125

LISA HUBBARD: 4, 7 (bottom), 16 (bottom left), 62-67

CHARLES MARAIA: 90 (bottom)

MARIA ROBLEDO: 19 (top left)

DAVID SAWYER: 37, 101, 116, 117, 122, 123

MATTHEW SEPTIMUS: 9 (bottom)

SIMON WATSON: 5, 6 (bottom center, bottom right), 7 (top right), 10, 11, 48-51, 53-59, 94 (top left, bottom right), 96 (bottom right), 97 (bottom left), 126

ANNA WILLIAMS: 2, 6 (middle left), 7 (top left), 17, 42-47, 60, 69, 70, 71 (top), 81, 82 (top, bottom center and right), 83, 85-89, 90 (top), 91-93, 94 (top right, bottom left), 95, 99, 100, 120

ILLUSTRATIONS

HARRY BATES: 85, 87, 98

INDEX